HANDLING EARTHLY TREASURE
BIBLICAL CERTAINTIES ABOUT MONEY

ALAN PATTERSON

BOB JONES
UNIVERSITY PRESS

Greenville, South Carolina

Library of Congress Cataloging-in-Publication Data

Patterson, Alan, 1953-
  Handling earthly treasure : biblical certainties about money / Alan Patterson.
      p. cm.
  Summary: "Explains what the Bible teaches about money"—Provided by publisher.
  Includes bibliographical references.
  ISBN 978-1-60682-214-2 (perfect bound pbk. : alk. paper)
  1. Money—Biblical teaching. 2. Money—Religious aspects—Christianity. I. Title.
  BS680.M57P38 2011
  220.8'3324—dc23
                          2011025342

BWHEBB, BWGRKL: BWHEBB, BWHEBL, BWTRANSH [Hebrew]; BWGRKL, BW-GRKN, and BWGRKI [Greek] Postscript® Type 1 and TrueTypeT fonts Copyright © 1994–2006 BibleWorks, LLC. All rights reserved. These Biblical Greek and Hebrew fonts are used with permission and are from BibleWorks, software for Biblical exegesis and research.

All Scripture is quoted from the Authorized King James Version unless otherwise noted.

NASB: Scripture taken from the NEW AMERICAN STANDARD BIBLE®, Copyright © 1960, 1962, 1963, 1968, 1971, 1972, 1973, 1975, 1977, 1995 by The Lockman Foundation. Used by permission.

The fact that materials produced by other publishers may be referred to in this volume does not constitute an endorsement of the content or theological position of materials produced by such publishers.

Handling Earthly Treasure: Biblical Certainties about Money
Alan Patterson, PhD

Design and page layout by Nathan Hutcheon

© 2011 by BJU Press
Greenville, South Carolina 29614

Bob Jones University Press is a division of BJU Press

Printed in the United States of America
All rights reserved

ISBN 978-1-60682-214-2

15   14   13   12   11   10   9   8   7   6   5   4   3   2   1

I dedicate this book to my wife, Jan.
Her commitment to these biblical principles has made it a joy
to strive together to handle our "earthly treasure"
in a God-honoring way.

CONTENTS

List of Abbreviations

KD...........C. F. Keil and Franz Delitzsch, *Biblical Commentary on the Old Testament*. Trans. James Martin. 25 vols. Edinburgh: T. & T. Clark, 1864-1901.

NASB ......New American Standard Bible.

TWOT.....Gleason Archer, R. Laird Harris, Bruce Waltke, eds., *Theological Wordbook of the Old Testament*. Chicago: Moody, 1980.

ZPEB ....Merrill C. Tenney, ed., *The Zondervan Pictorial Encyclopedia of the Bible*. Grand Rapids: Zondervan, 1975-76.

INTRODUCTION

The godly stewardship of one's possessions is as much a Christian's responsibility as his parenting, his work ethic, or any other aspect of holy living. Some conclude that because Christ Himself referred to mammon as "unrighteous," we must avoid dealing with it or even thinking about it. That is a misguided approach. The fact is that the Lord has given us much information and numerous guiding principles about the proper use of our wealth, whether significant or meager. The person who desires to please the Lord in everything will have to make decisions about such things as financial planning, giving, being indebted, owning property, making money in a business, and even responding to poverty. One can find radical advice in nearly all of these areas, and some of that advice derives from Bible texts. However, the extreme positions nearly always fail to take into account the full biblical picture. This book will attempt to examine many of those positions in the light of the full scope of biblical revelation. Though not specifically a book of financial advice, it is intended to guide the reader into wise decisions in critical areas of money use.

Every generation knows what it is like to go through at least one recession. During those times most of us have understood that things were tight financially and that no investments were truly safe. With no effort God can blow away the richest man's wealth and leave him destitute. If nothing else, financial meltdowns, stock market drops, and job losses show us that trusting wealth or the ability to get wealth is utterly foolish. However, knowing the instability of wealth does not exempt us from handling money issues. On the contrary, the uncertainties of money make it even more important for believers to set their financial house in order. After looking at the Bible's teaching, we may determine that we should save more. Or we may become convinced that we should give more. We certainly should determine to do everything we can to get out of and stay out of debt. We should also come to a better awareness of how to define and how to relate to the poverty in the world.

1

The Right Use of Money: Financial Planning

George Müller refused to lay money aside for his own future needs. Biographer A. T. Pierson explains Müller's conviction against laying up funds for old age, future illnesses, or emergencies:

> He had settled the matter beyond raising the question again, that he would live from day to day upon the Lord's bounty, and would make but *one investment*, namely, using whatever means God gave, to supply the necessities of the poor, depending on God richly to repay him in the hour of his own need, according to the promise: 'He that hath pity upon the poor lendeth unto the Lord, and that which he hath given will He pay him again' (Pr. 19:17).[1]

Müller also said, "Let no one profess to trust God and yet lay up for future wants; otherwise the Lord will send him to the hoard he has amassed, before he can answer the prayer for more."[2] His words imply that all saving for future wants eliminates the possibility of trusting God and therefore is wrong. John Wesley made similar statements in his preaching. For instance, in his sermon on the "Danger of Increasing Riches," he states: "Hoard nothing. Lay up no treasure on earth, but 'give all you can,' that is, all you have.

---

[1] *A. T. Pierson, George Müller of Bristol* (Old Tappan, NJ: Revell, n.d.), 341.
[2] Ibid., 442.

I defy all the men upon earth, yea, all the angels in heaven, to find any other way of extracting the poison from riches."[3]

If Müller and Wesley are correct in their rebuke of having a surplus, that is, if their thinking harmonizes with all of the biblical data, then this chapter, which advocates judicious saving and investing, has no merit for the Christian. However, further treatment will show that Müller's and Wesley's persuasion does not represent all of the biblical data. Müller's conviction is noteworthy because he claimed a biblical basis for it, because he lived by it, and because the Lord honored it. Nevertheless, although the Bible warns against storing up treasures on earth instead of in heaven (Matt. 6:19–20), it also enjoins wise financial planning. The Christian does not necessarily annul his faith by judiciously providing for future needs. In fact, making proper financial plans is a major responsibility for the Christian.

If for no other reason, the Christian should have financial plans because common sense requires it. Jesus suggested the wisdom of planning in Luke 14:28 and 31—to start to build a tower but then to leave off with only the foundation laid is to invite ridicule. To go to battle undermanned is also foolish. Counting the cost of these undertakings is imperative if one would avoid insult and derision (v. 29). Therefore, common sense requires that one take forethought before beginning anything that will require resources. Though these verses are not primarily about financial planning, they certainly suggest the wisdom of such forethought even in the realm of economics. The believer must plan so that his income will

---

[3] Albert C. Outler, ed., *Sermons IV: 115–151*, vol. 4, *The Works of John Wesley* (Nashville: Abingdon Press, 1987), 185. We should note that in another of his sermons on "The Use of Money," Wesley seems to allow that leaving an inheritance can be acceptable, though even here he warns against leaving an inheritance to those who will abuse it. *Sermons II: 34–70*, vol. 2, *The Works of John Wesley* (Nashville: Abingdon Press, 1985), 276.

cover his outlay; otherwise, he will end up with an embarrassing disaster. Besides the general observation that planning for future resource needs is wise, the Scriptures also delineate more explicitly the Christian's responsibilities for such planning.

BENEFICIARIES

A natural question for the believer is who should benefit from his planning, and we can be thankful that the Bible clearly explains who the primary beneficiaries should be. Besides himself, the Christian is chiefly responsible to consider his immediate family and then other relatives when making financial plans. As an analysis of pertinent verses will show, the responsibility is not a light one.

Immediate Family

In Old Testament times the wise father made provision for his children. In his directions to the polygamous man about the right of primogeniture,[4] Moses said,

> If a man has two wives, the one loved and the other unloved, and both the loved and the unloved have borne him sons, if the first-born son belongs to the unloved, then it shall be in the day he wills what he has to his sons, he cannot make the son of the loved the firstborn before the son of the unloved, who is the firstborn (Deut. 21:15–16, NASB).

> The proposed action by the father was equivalent to making a will,[5] although the ancient Israelites probably knew

---

[4] The right of primogeniture was the right of the firstborn son (oldest son of all wives) to receive an inheritance double that of the other sons. See Gen. 24:36; 25:5; Deut. 21:17.

[5] Peter C. Craigie, *The Book of Deuteronomy* (Grand Rapids: Eerdmans, 1976), 283. See also Roland de Vaux, *Ancient Israel*, trans., John McHugh (New York: McGraw-Hill, 1961), 53.

nothing of a written will. The father's dividing the inheritance was his way to provide for his children. If nothing else, such planning forced him to provide impartially for his children.

That the father would leave an inheritance to his children was assumed in Old Testament times. For example, when David exhorted the Israelites to possess their promised land, he assumed that they would perpetually "bequeath" it to their sons (1 Chron. 28:8, NASB). Similarly, Ezra described Israel's continuously leaving the land to her descendants as meeting the approval of God (Ezra 9:12). Solomon was even clearer. Under divine inspiration he maintained that "a good man leaveth an inheritance to his children's children: and the wealth of the sinner is laid up for the just" (Prov. 13:22). The "good" man is either the generous man or the morally upright man.[6] "Good" probably refers to the morally upright or righteous man, because this rendering emphasizes the contrast between the good man and the sinner. Therefore, the verse teaches that God may bless the morally good man with prosperity because of his conformity to God's law.[7] The good man will not squander his God-given wealth but will use at least part of it as a bequest to his children and grandchildren. A good man knows how to use wealth in a good way. His wealth places him in the "favorable circumstance of being able to help others."[8] As Solomon said further, "House and riches are the inheritance of fathers" (Prov. 19:14a).

---

[6] *KD, Proverbs*, 1:285, suggests generous; Crawford H. Toy, *A Critical and Exegetical Commentary on the Book of Proverbs* (Edinburgh: T. and T. Clark, 1970), 276, suggests morally upright.

[7] Toy, 276.

[8] Bruce K. Waltke, *The Book of Proverbs: Chapters 1–15* (Grand Rapids: Eerdmans, 2004), 572.

Paul also suggested the need to provide for children with his affirmation of fatherly love for the Corinthians: "Behold, the third time I am ready to come to you; and I will not be burdensome to you: for I seek not yours, but you: for the children ought not to lay up for the parents, but the parents for the children" (2 Cor. 12:14). In this context, where Paul emphasizes his parental love for his spiritual children, he assumes the truthfulness of the concept that parents should make a concerted effort not only to provide for their children's present needs but also to "lay up" for their future needs.[9] This word is the very word used in Matthew 6:19–20, where Jesus warned about the evil of hoarding and which Müller and others have used to categorically condemn saving money. But the complete biblical view must include this balancing statement by Paul, who accepted as a principle of nature that parents will treasure up provisions for their children.[10] Storing up wealth for his children is not only the parent's privilege, but his duty. He is obligated to do so if he can.[11] Tasker claims that it was particularly important for the parent in Paul's day to lay up for his children, since no "welfare state" existed.[12] He is right, but the obligation still stands. The Christian parent who can work should not depend upon the state to care for his children.

Other Relatives

The Christian should plan not only for the needs of his children, but also for the needs of other family members. Paul is unequivocal about this obligation: "But if any provide not for his own, and

---

[9] "To lay up" translates θησαυρίζω. It denotes to store up, or to accumulate, for use at a later time. See its use in Luke 12:21 where it describes the action of the foolish man who stores up enough goods to live on for "many years" (Luke 12:19).

[10] Charles Hodge, *An Exposition of the Second Epistle to the Corinthians* (1859; repr., Grand Rapids: Baker, 1980), 293.

[11] He "ought" to. The verb ὀφείλω means "to be obligated."

[12] R. V. G. Tasker, *The Second Epistle of Paul to the Corinthians* (Grand Rapids: Eerdmans, 1977), 182.

specially for those of his own house, he hath denied the faith, and is worse than an infidel" (1 Tim. 5:8). Paul enjoins broad duties on the Christian man. Generally the Christian must provide for "his own." That is, he must provide for all his servants as well as his family members.[13] But above all, the Christian must provide for his own family members.[14] A Christian has a particular obligation to his relatives when they need support. One's own "house" may include distant relatives as well as immediate family.[15] In order to fulfill this Christian duty, one must give it ample forethought. But this command also requires continuous attention to the responsibility.[16] That is, the Christian man must make financial plans that will enable him to provide for the needs of his servants and relatives. Of course, he has no obligation to provide for those who can provide for themselves (2 Thess. 3:10). But as much as he is able,

---

[13] R. C. H. Lenski, *The Interpretation of St. Paul's Epistles to the Colossians, to the Thessalonians, to Timothy, to Titus, and to Philemon* (Minneapolis: Augsburg Publishing House, 1961), 663. William Hendriksen thinks the reference is more indefinite, possibly including friends. *New Testament Commentary: Exposition of the Pastoral Epistles* (Grand Rapids: Baker, 1957), 171. The reference is indefinite, but it probably does not include friends. Paul is going from the general ("his own") to the specific ("those of his own house"). Therefore, he envisions only one large group, including both slaves and family, with a subgroup, including only family. Lenski (663) points out that the one article τῶν applies to both words, ἰδίων ("his own") and οἰκείων ("house" or "kindred"). The Twentieth Century New Testament translates the phrase "those under his own roof."

[14] Paul may especially have in mind a Christian's providing for his aged parents. See Guy H. King's *A Leader Led* for a development of this view. (Wheaton: Van Kampen Press, 1951), 89–90.

[15] Albert Barnes takes "his own" as a reference to "all who are naturally dependent on him. . . . There may be many distant relatives naturally dependent on our aid." *Notes on the New Testament: Thessalonians, Timothy, Titus and Philemon*, ed. Robert Frew (Grand Rapids: Baker, 1977), 176.

[16] The word "provide" (προνοέω) literally means to "think of beforehand." Louw defines the word as "to care for or look after, with the implication of continuous responsibility." J. Louw and E. A. Nida, *Vol. 1: Greek-English Lexicon of the New Testament: Based on Semantic Domains* (electronic ed. of the 2nd edition) (New York: United Bible Societies, 1996), 462.

the Christian head of the house must lay aside funds for those of his kindred who will need support.

The believer cannot regard this obligation lightly. If he fails to meet it, he "denies the faith" and becomes worse than one who has no faith. To fail to plan provisions for one's needy servants or relatives is to manifest a fatal flaw in one's obedience to "the faith," the rule of life which is based on obedience to the law of love. The kind of faith possessed by genuine Christians "must of necessity express itself in acts of loving kindness."[17] But to claim to have such faith, and yet to flagrantly deny it in practice, is much worse than to make no pretence. Hypocrisy is a terrible sin. But the Christian who will not make provision for his relatives is further blameworthy because even non-Christians have recognized the responsibility to provide for their kindred. Therefore, the professing Christian who neglects this duty evinces a moral standard lower than that of an unbeliever. As White rightly observes, "The Christian who falls below the best heathen standard of family affection is more the blameworthy, since he has, what the heathen has not, the supreme example of love in Jesus Christ."[18]

Planning for the future, then, is not only proper, but it is incumbent upon the Christian. One need that demands such planning is that of providing for one's family and relatives. The Christian must honor his parents (Eph. 6:2–3); sometimes that honoring requires providing support. If it does, the Christian must be quick and willing to do so.[19] However, one's ability to provide for needy

---

[17] Robert H. Mounce, *Pass It On* (Glendale, CA: Regal Books, 1979), 70.

[18] Newport J. O. White, *The First and Second Epistles to Timothy and the Epistle to Titus*, in *The Expositor's Greek Testament*, ed. W. Robertson Nicoll, vol. 4 (New York: George H. Doran, n.d.), 129.

[19] Jesus implied this in his condemnation of the Pharisees and scribes for not supporting their parents (Mark 7:11). They were using a pious vow, "That by which you might have been helped by me is Corban!" to state that the financial gift they had would be dedicated to supporting the temple and therefore could not be used for other

relatives depends upon the amount of financial planning and setting aside of funds done ahead of time. Therefore, the fulfillment of the duty that Paul urges requires forethought and financial planning.

AREAS

The three major areas of financial planning are spending, investing, and saving. All are equally important, because mismanagement in one area eventually, if not immediately, affects the other two areas.

Spending

The Christian must avoid spending foolishly. As Solomon says, "There is treasure to be desired and oil in the dwelling of the wise; but a foolish man spendeth it up" (Prov. 21:20). Foolish spending has many causes, and although financial planning will not remedy all of them, it will help. Living only for the present, the fool is not interested in planning for the future. He prefers to ignore the future and to squander ("spendeth up" literally means to "swallow up"; see Gen. 41:7 and Num. 16:32) his money selfishly. The fool needs financial planning, but more than that, he needs a change in character. Implicit in Solomon's statement is that along with a change in the fool's character will come a tendency to handle money wisely. The wise man, and specifically here the one who has wise financial plans, will normally have an abundance of funds. There will be "precious treasure" (NASB) and "oil" in his house. Therefore, the fool needs wise financial planning, for it automatically curbs foolish spending. What the foolish person loses through rapid consuming the wise person gains through careful planning and self-control.

---

purposes such as financially assisting parents. In other words, by simply calling a gift "Corban" they could rid themselves of any financial obligation to their parents and even appear pious in doing so.

Financial planning is indeed necessary if the believer is to avoid foolish spending. The Christian must be the opposite of the foolish man, who, rather than planning the use of his money, can hardly wait to spend it.[20] When he plans wisely, the believer will often have a surplus. Barnes rightly observes that "the wise man keeps a store in reserve. He gains uprightly, spends moderately, [and] never exhausts himself."[21]

Investing

The Lord expects Christians to be good stewards with the money He gives them. Nowhere is the divine approval of wisely investing money seen more clearly than in the parable of the talents (Matt. 25:14–30).[22] The parable is much more than an exhortation to wise investment. But the same law of diligence applies whether the parable refers to the use of money or to the use of spiritual gifts.[23] The general theme of this parable is an exhortation to the improvement of everything that God gives, whether it be money, time, opportunity, or natural talents. Nevertheless, Christ's use of the monetary framework implies His approval of wise trading and investing.

Upon receiving their talents, two of the servants invested them and made other talents (Matt. 25:16–17).[24] In other words, they

---

[20] W. Gunther Plaut, *Book of Proverbs* (New York: Union of American Hebrew Congregations, 1961), 222.

[21] Albert Barnes, *The Bible Commentary*, ed. F. C. Cook (Grand Rapids: Baker, 1977), 60.

[22] Compare the similar but distinct parable of the ten pounds in Luke 19:11–27.

[23] A. B. Bruce, *The Synoptic Gospels*, in *The Expositor's Greek Testament*, ed. W. Robertson Nicoll, vol. 1 (New York: George H. Doran, n.d.), 304.

[24] "The 'talent' . . . was not a coin, but a measure or weight of money, which was sometimes paid in minted coins and sometimes in bars of gold or bullion." R. V. G. Tasker, *The Gospel According to St. Matthew* (Grand Rapids: Eerdmans, 1961), 235. Therefore, the exact value varied, depending on the type of coin measured out.

"put to work"[25] the money and "made a profit."[26] Jesus' approval (vv. 21, 23), rather than censure, of their profit-making is noteworthy since He often reproached the rich (e.g., Mark 10:23; Luke 6:24; 12:13–21). The difference is that here Jesus applauds diligence and wise stewardship, whereas in the other references He condemns trust in money. According to Jesus' words, even a feeble attempt at making a profit is better than fearfully neglecting capital (vv. 26–30). In summary, Jesus teaches that those who do not improve their God-given assets may lose them (v. 28). God gives money to His servants according to each one's ability to manage it.[27] He expects them to use their wealth in ways that glorify Him, that promote His kingdom, and that benefit His children.[28] Therefore, the Christian should plan to put his money to work, not to amass a hoard, but to use the proceeds for his Master's glory.

The master's words to the unjust steward also imply that Christians should be astute stewards of God's provisions (Luke 16:10–12). The topic of these verses is clearly money. Therefore, a major, if not the primary, application has to do with one's use of money. One's handling of money can serve as a sort of spiritual barometer because it indicates the quality of one's Christian stewardship.[29] In fact, Luke implies that unfaithfulness in the use of "unrighteous mammon" confirms one's incapacity to manage wisely spiritual bestowments.[30] The "least" thing (v. 10) is that material wealth,

---

[25] "Traded" is from ἐργάζομαι ("to work").

[26] Each servant "gained" (from κερδαίνω, vv. 17, 20) from his business transactions.

[27] He gave to each servant "according to his own ability" (v. 15, NASB).

[28] William Hendriksen, *New Testament Commentary: Exposition of the Gospel According to Matthew* (Grand Rapids: Baker, 1973), 884.

[29] John F. MacArthur, Jr., *Giving: God's Way* (Wheaton: Tyndale House Publishers, 1978), 18.

[30] The epithet "unrighteous mammon" does not mean that money is inherently evil. It simply connotes the unrighteous attitudes and practices often associated with the acquiring and using of money. It serves to warn the Christian to be honest in acquiring and careful in using money.

which in reality God owns, but which has in varying degrees fallen into human control. But that least thing reveals much. For how one acquires and uses wealth demonstrates one's character. Clearly God expects the Christian to be a faithful and wise steward in the ordinary aspects of life, which include investing money. The proper handling of money is serious business. MacArthur is right: "The credibility of your Christianity is manifest in the handling of your funds."[31]

Saving

The Christian expects and can even partially predict periods of meager financial resources. Other times, such as emergencies, he expects occasionally but cannot predict. Nevertheless the Christian can plan in general ways for emergencies. Therefore the Christian should take steps to plan for both anticipated lean times and emergencies.

Anticipated Lean Times

The example of Joseph well illustrates the wisdom of storing up for lean times (Gen. 41:37–57). Joseph, applying his understanding of Pharaoh's dreams, stored up one fifth of each year's produce (41:14–36). Because he did this for seven years, his people had food during the years of famine (41:54). In fact, the Egyptians had food to spare for all the countries round about them (41:56–57). A key aspect of Joseph's example is his diligence in carrying out his plan for storing up. Financial planning is no good if not carried out. Knowing this necessity for execution and knowing that the people themselves would probably not save voluntarily, Joseph took charge and appointed officials (41:34) to superintend the storage procedure.[32] Joseph foresaw the danger to those under

---

[31] MacArthur, 47.

[32] George Bush points out that the Egyptians probably would not have saved on their own. *Notes on Genesis*, vol. 2 (1860; repr., New York: James and Klock, 1976),

his charge if he did not formulate and execute proper planning. He knew that forethought coupled with execution was the best strategy against famine.

Like Joseph, Solomon was a wise ruler who planned for the lean times that his people might encounter. Solomon's plan was to build "cities of store" (1 Kings 9:19) to hold the agricultural surpluses. This surplus of produce supplied the army, the rural population, and sometimes even travelers and their animals.[33] The main reason for these store-cities was to provide the necessities of food and oil during times of famine or war.[34] Of course, these provisions were always available, apart from famine and war.

Other leaders also recognized the importance of storing for hard times. Pharaoh built the store-cities of Pithom and Raamses (Exod. 1:11). Jehoshaphat built cities of store as part of his effort to strengthen Judah (2 Chron. 17:12).[35] Hezekiah built "storehouses" for the main products of the land—"grain, wine and oil" (2 Chron. 32:28, NASB).

Strange as it may seem, Solomon reinforced this lesson about diligent planning and execution with the indefatigable ant. In his inspired collection of Proverbs, Solomon exhorted the reader to "go to the ant" in order to learn from a careful observation of "her ways" (6:6). The ant is commendable for two main reasons. First, she has "'no guide' to direct her work, no 'overseer' to inspect her,

---

282; such a procedure was not uncommon in Egypt. According to John Skinner, "State granaries, for the sustenance of the army, the officials and the serfs, were a standing feature of Egyptian administration." *A Critical and Exegetical Commentary on Genesis*, 2nd ed. (Edinburgh: T. and T. Clark, 1976), 472.

[33] *KD, Kings*, 145.

[34] Oil was used for cooking, for lamp fuel, for medicinal purposes, and even for religious rituals. R. K. H[arrison], "Oil," *The Illustrated Bible Dictionary*, (1980), 2:1111; *KD, Kings*, 145.

[35] H[arvey] E. Finley, "Store-Cities," *ZPEB* (1975), 5:524.

and no 'ruler' to call her to account" (6:7),[36] but she works hard and efficiently anyway. Secondly, and more importantly for this discussion, she "provideth her meat in the summer, and gathereth her food in the harvest" (6:8). Knowing that winter is coming, when it may be impossible for her to gather food, she stores up appropriate provisions during the harvest season.[37] As Agur says later in Proverbs, "The ants are a people not strong, yet they prepare their meat in the summer" (30:25). Again, the obvious implication is that she prepares for the lean wintertime by laying up in the summer.[38] The lesson from the ant then is simple: "provide for the bad times during good times."[39]

The industrious planning of the ant incriminates the slothful man. The indolent man, who loves sleep (6:9–11), has less character than the diminutive "model of unwearied and well-planned labour."[40] The ant's assiduous planning illustrates well the need to lay up for anticipated lean times. The results of proper planning are blessed. Just as the ant will enjoy comfort and plenty in the dead of winter while other creatures suffer cold and hunger, so the wise financial planner will have enough lean-time provision for those under his charge. However, the result of failing to store up industriously for hard times is not pleasant. Solomon described this result frankly: "Your poverty will come in like a vagabond and your need like an armed man" (6:11, NASB).[41] Poverty will assault the sluggard like

---

[36] Charles Bridges, *A Commentary on Proverbs* (1846; repr., Carlisle, PA: The Banner of Truth Trust, 1974), 61.

[37] "Summer" and "harvest" (v. 8) mean essentially the same thing. Both are general references to the harvest season, which may last from March (for barley, 2 Sam. 21:9) to September (for grapes, Isa. 18:5). Toy, 124.

[38] Ibid., 534.

[39] Duane A. Garrett, *Proverbs, Ecclesiastes, Song of Songs*, vol. 14, *The New American Commentary* (Nashville: Broadman Press, 1993), 242.

[40] *KD, Proverbs*, 1:140.

[41] Cf. 24:30–34.

a "strong robber" and will overwhelm him before he can make a defense.[42] Clearly, financial planning coupled with industriousness is much better than unexpected poverty. There can be no denying it: "He that gathereth [for a future store][43] in summer is a wise son: but he that sleepeth in harvest is a son that causeth shame" (10:5).

Emergencies

The Christian cannot prepare for every kind of emergency. In fact, the Lord often causes emergencies in order that Christians may learn where their trust really lies. Nevertheless, financial planning that recognizes the likelihood of emergencies is not wrong for the Christian. Two references in Proverbs suggest that such planning is important, if not imperative.

In the first reference, Solomon affirms that "the thoughts of the diligent tend only to plenteousness; but of every one that is hasty only to want" (21:5). Unlike the hasty man, the diligent man will plan and reflect upon his work.[44] The result of diligence and planning will be "plenteousness," that is, an abundance that leaves an excess after necessities are provided.[45] The diligent man may legitimately use part of the surplus of God's blessing upon his labor as a hedge against emergencies.

"A prudent man foreseeth the evil, and hideth himself: but the simple pass on, and are punished" (22:3; cf. 27:12). Throughout Proverbs the "prudent man" is one with positive character.[46] He is

---

[42] *KD, Proverbs*, 1:141.

[43] Ibid., 212.

[44] "Thoughts" (KJV) translates the word מַחֲשָׁבוֹת. This word sometimes means "plans." The NASB translates it "plans." And *TWOT*, 1:330, gives this as one meaning. It comes from the root חָשַׁב, which most commonly denotes the formulation of new ideas, or planning. Ibid.

[45] Ibid., 420.

[46] He is calm in the face of insult (12:16; Toy, 252), slow to broadcast his knowledge (12:23), deliberate to act according to his knowledge (13:16), careful to understand where he is going (14:8, 15), and "crowned with knowledge" (14:18).

particularly careful to scout the road before him and to strive to make his journey pleasing to God. He is not naïve. He recognizes his responsibility to plan for the future. Therefore, he is always looking ahead to foresee evil, in order that he might avoid it. In short, he is a "man of forethought."[47] In accordance with his practical knowledge of life's facts, the prudent man makes plans to "turn aside" from distressing situations of every kind. Therefore, when he foresees the likelihood of financial distress, he makes plans to avoid it.[48]

SUMMARY

The Christian has a solemn obligation to make financial plans. Those plans should focus on providing for the needs of his family. Of course, not every Christian can provide for his children's or his relatives' future needs. The best he can do in some circumstances is to leave a "good name" for his family.[49] A righteous man has the assurance that God will provide for his descendants (Ps. 37:25). Most people understand that one can even hurt his children or relatives by leaving them an inheritance in excess of their needs.[50] But in spite of the attendant problems, the Christian must make plans to provide for "his own" (1 Tim. 5:8). Besides providing for his immediate and distant kindred, the Christian should also plan for financial lean times. The ant provides a vivid illustration of this stewardship (Prov. 6:6–11, 30:25). In order to fulfill these

---

[47] Toy, 414.

[48] Toy (414) says that "evil" is "anything which is a source of injury, financial [emphasis added], physical or moral."

[49] A reputation for upright character is much better than riches (Prov. 22:1).

[50] One of the world's richest men, Bill Gates, has reportedly taken this into account in determining how to divide his wealth. In answer to the question about why he was giving away his money, Gates told interviewer George Stephanopoulus "Well, the first thing was the decision that it probably would not be good for my kids, for it to go to them. . . . They'll get something but not a substantial percentage" (http://abcnews. go.com/ThisWeek/GlobalHealth/story?id=1286093).

duties, the Christian must avoid foolish spending but cultivate wise investment. Assuredly, God will honor him who dutifully plans and administers his wealth.[51] Although God expects believers to use and even accumulate money for specified purposes, one cannot conclude that the goal should be to become rich. Coupled with the recognition of the proper place of and use for money are numerous biblical cautions about money. In the next chapter we will consider many of these cautions.

---

[51] The parable of the ten virgins (Matt. 25:1–13) teaches that God honors those who think ahead. The five virgins who took reserves of oil for their nocturnal procession understood the importance of planning ahead. They were rewarded with entrance to the wedding (v. 10).

2

CAUTIONS ABOUT THE WRONG USE OF MONEY

Have you ever heard someone misquote 1 Timothy 6:10 by saying that "money is the root of all evil"? Or how about this misrepresentation of the biblical teaching on wealth:

> The problem, according to the Old Testament, is the accumulation of wealth and the oppression of the poor. The New Testament carries the theme further, regarding the very possession of wealth as a fundamental spiritual problem; for wealth distorts people's priorities, makes them insensitive to others, and seriously obstructs their relationship to God.[1]

Many people seem to believe the misquotation of 1 Timothy 6:10, but the truth is that *not* money itself, but the "love of money" leads to all kinds of evil attitudes and practices. Others such as Jim Wallis have grossly overstated the cautions about money. We need to remember what we learned in the previous chapter: God will honor the faithful administrator of wealth. However, the genuinely faithful stewardship of one's wealth is no easy task. Some of the biblical cautions for financial planning are so alarming that meeting the obligation to plan, while also heeding the cautions, seems almost impossible. Indeed, the task does demand much prayerful thought, godly advice, and honest evaluation of motives. One cannot be a good steward of the resources God gives him

---

[1] Jim Wallis, *The Call to Conversion* (New York: Harper and Row, 1981), 59.

without taking heed to biblical warnings and cautions about the improper pursuit and use of money.

GET-RICH-QUICK SCHEMES

Although the Christian may legitimately invest his money, he may not legitimately invest in get-rich-quick schemes. The Scriptures forbid this kind of investment, by which one is hoping to "strike it rich."[2] The apparent success of others may motivate a person to choose risky investments. But the Psalmist admonishes, "Rest in the Lord, and wait patiently for him: fret not thyself because of him who prospereth in his way, because of the man who bringeth wicked devices to pass" (Ps. 37:7). Oftentimes the wicked prosper because they use dishonest plans and schemes. But the Christian can have no part in such plots. His response to enticing, speculative investments must always be one of patient waiting for the Lord's clear leading and one of confidence in His provision. The Christian will have no problem with speculative financial schemes if he remembers that "wealth gotten by vanity ["fraud," NASB] shall be diminished: but he that gathereth by labor shall increase" (Prov. 13:11).[3] The Scripture writer here skillfully uses the word "vanity" to indicate not only that the means of acquiring can be evil, but also that the wealth acquired by such means is worthless in the sight of God; it is empty of meaning.[4] Waltke helpfully describes the writer's intent:

---

[2] Larry Burkett, *The Stewardship of Investments* (Norcross, GA: Christian Financial Concepts, 1978), 1. Because all business enterprises involve some risk, risk is inherent in any investment. Therefore, as the following treatment will show, an investment becomes a get-rich-quick scheme, not when an investor assumes some risk, but when his motivation is that of greed, or when he invests hastily, without an accurate knowledge of the facts or the Lord's will.

[3] *KD, Proverbs*, 1:276, explains "vanity" as "morally unrestrained fraudulent and deceitful speculation."

[4] The word suggests emptiness and impermanence and is often translated "vapor," "breath," or "futility."

The metaphor of getting money from a vapor suggests what English speakers call "easy money," including tyranny, injustice, extortion, lies and windfalls, at the expense of others. . . . Instead of these "windy" methods, the book prescribes the substantial methods of patience, diligence, prudence, generosity, and faith, virtues that have stood the test of time.[5]

Self-confessed Ponzi scheme[6] expert Bernie Madoff is seeing the truth of this verse play out as he spends time in jail for bilking his clients. The wealth he got by his vanity has vanished, and so has much of that of his trusting clients. A *New York Times* article about him was entitled "The 17th Floor, Where Wealth Went to Vanish."[7]

Solomon also warned about risky investments that are made hastily because of a possibly high return.[8] He says, "The thoughts of the diligent tend only to plenteousness; but of every one that is hasty only to want ["poverty," NASB]" (Prov. 21:5). Haste, rarely wise, is particularly unwise in money matters.[9] The usual result of haste is not great earnings, but grievous "poverty." The patient, plodding work of the diligent man will bring better returns than the "undisciplined impulse" of the man hasting after riches.[10] Financial advisor Larry Burkett offers sound advice: "Never get

---

[5] Bruce K. Waltke, *The Book of Proverbs: Chapters 1–15*, 561.

[6] A Ponzi scheme is a fraudulent plan whereby investors are paid "profits" from the investments of other investors rather than from actual return on their money. Eventually the supply of new investors dries up, and the last investors not only see no profit but lose their entire investment.

[7] Diana B. Henriques and Alex Berenson, *The New York Times*, 14 December, 2008, Section A, 1.

[8] Derek Kidner makes the theme of Prov. 21:5–6 "get-rich-quick." *The Proverbs* (Downers Grove, IL: InterVarsity Press, 1964), 142.

[9] Cf. Prov. 20:21, "An inheritance may be gotten hastily at the beginning; but the end thereof shall not be blessed."

[10] Bridges, *Proverbs*, 369.

involved in financial decisions that require instant action, but allow God to take His course."[11]

Solomon continues the theme in 28:20, where he assures us that "a faithful man will abound with blessings, but he who makes haste to be rich will not go unpunished" (NASB). He goes on to observe that "a man with an evil eye hastens after wealth and does not know that want will come upon him" (28:22, NASB). The first reference levels solemn warning against attempts at quick dollars. The consequences of such attempts are certain—the greedy[12] man will not be "free from guilt,"[13] and hence will not escape punishment.[14] The second reference depicts the hasty man as one with an "evil eye." This idiom substantiates the thought that greed motivates the hasty man. One who is "evil of eye" (lit.) is a "selfish man" (23:6, NASB), a greedy man, whose envy of the prosperity of others causes him to strive passionately for their height of affluence.[15] In the context such a man is one who "follows empty pursuits" (28:19, NASB), which "could be unprofitable occupations or business speculations."[16]

In summary, the desire to get rich hastily is wrong for the Christian. "An inheritance" (or any other financial surplus) "gotten hastily" will almost certainly "not be blessed" (Prov. 20:21).[17]

---

[11] *The Complete Guide to Managing Your Money* (New York: Inspirational Press, 1996), 62.

[12] Greed is probably the stimulus that makes the man hasty. See Bridges' discussion, 546–47.

[13] Toy, *Proverbs*, 503.

[14] Cf. 6:29, 11:21, 16:5, 17:5, 19:5, and 19:9, where the same Hebrew idiom, "he will not go unpunished," is used.

[15] *KD, Proverbs*, 2:236.

[16] Garrett, *Proverbs, Ecclesiastes, Song of Songs*, 226.

[17] This verse cannot be taken to contradict other biblical teaching on leaving an inheritance to one's children. (See earlier discussion.) But with the inheritance should come instruction on how to use it wisely, following all the biblical principles discussed in this book.

One's life savings can easily dissipate in a get-rich-quick enter-prise.[18] The Christian with an inordinate desire to be rich will "fall into temptation and a snare and many foolish and harmful desires which plunge men into ruin and destruction" (1 Tim. 6:9, NASB). Therefore, he must beware of attempting to make money from high-risk investments. Such attempts border on gambling. Whereas the gambler takes delight in the element of chance, the Christian should seek to minimize risk.[19] The Christian can never legitimately take great risks with life or money unless his choice to do so issues from "something other than . . . the thrill of a meaningless adventure," or a greedy desire for more money.[20]

A word about lotteries and gambling is in order here. Gambling is defined as "a contract whereby the loss or gain of something of value is made wholly dependent on an uncertain event. If either of the contracting parties is in a state of certainty about the event, the gamble is invalid and fraudulent. The common forms of a gamble are bets, games of chance, and lotteries."[21] Such things as games without stakes or bets, sweepstakes give-aways that do not require payment, buying stocks, or buying insurance are not gambling, for uncompensated losses are not at issue. A person may do those things out of greed or discontent or with other wrong motives, but his problem is not an issue of gambling.[22] In other words, a

---

[18] Larry Burkett, *Your Finances in Changing Times* (n.p.: Christian Financial Concepts, 1975), 69.

[19] That the rate of return on an investment is almost always proportional to its risk is a well-established fact. Therefore, the more risk one is willing to take, the greater the possible rate of return, but also the greater the possibility of financial disaster. The biblical data demand conservatism in investing.

[20] Nolan B. Harmon, Jr., *Is It Right or Wrong?* (Nashville: Cokesbury Press, 1938), 102.

[21] F. L. Cross and E. A. Livingstone, *The Oxford Dictionary of the Christian Church*, 3rd ed. rev. (Oxford: Oxford University Press, 2005), 198.

[22] Numerous texts warn about greed (always desiring more) and covetousness (extreme desire for more, but especially for what belongs to another). See, for example,

"gambler always wants financial loss to occur, because he hopes to profit from those losses."[23]

Is gambling common, and is it a potential problem for Christians? Unfortunately, the answer seems to be a strong yes. The National Council on Problem Gambling reports that 85% of Americans have gambled at least once in their lifetimes, and 60% of Americans gamble each year. Legal gambling is available in every state except Hawaii and Utah. The revenues that these legal gambling places took in after the payouts were over $92 billion in 2007.[24] All of this is legal gambling; the amount of unauthorized gambling is no doubt far higher. With the problem so widespread, Christians are bound to be affected and tempted. The temptation occurs in the grocery store, in the office, in the clubhouse, and in places where casinos are legal. For instance, in many offices across America the euphemistic term "office pool" is used to mask the reality of the gambling going on. In many states the other euphemistic term, "lottery," is used to describe the way the state gets money for its programs by urging its citizens to gamble for the extremely unlikely possibility of winning the lottery. In other words, one does not have to go to Las Vegas or a casino to gamble, for any attempt to get money purely by paying for a chance drawing is gambling and seems to fall under God's condemnation of get-rich-quick schemes. Newheiser succinctly summarizes the problems of gambling:

> Gambling undermines the work ethic by encouraging people to hope for wealth without working for it (Pr. 28:19). Gambling promotes irrationality in that the odds against winning a large prize are astronomical (Pr. 14:23).

Prov. 11:6 (NASB); Luke 12:15; Eph. 5:3, 5; 2 Pet. 2:14.

[23] http://gospelway.com/morality/gambling.php.

[24] http://www.myaddiction.com/education/articles/gambling_statistics.html.

Gambling is motivated by a greedy lust for riches (Pr. 28:22, 20; 1 Tim. 6:6, 10). Gambling exploits those who lose (Pr. 22:16). Gambling has harmful effects on society in terms of increases in crime, substance abuse, debt, suicide, and the breakup of families. Gambling is poor stewardship of God's resources. Only two things can happen when you gamble, and both are bad: you may lose, which means you have foolishly wasted your money; or you may win, in which case you have defrauded others by taking their money without earning it.[25]

Office pool and lottery "winners" are losers in God's view. Remember, anything gained by "vanity" is sure to "be diminished" (Prov. 13:11). Christians can depend upon the Lord to provide all of their needs (Matt. 6:25–34). They must never resort to practices that will harm others to help themselves.

HOARDING

Although the Christian may legitimately save money, he may not legitimately hoard it.[26] The difference between storing up properly and hoarding is motive and focus. To hoard is to store up selfishly while neglecting one's relationship to God. Jesus directly warned against hoarding when He said,

> Lay not up for yourselves treasures upon earth, where moth and rust doth corrupt, and where thieves break through and steal: but lay up for yourselves treasures in heaven, where neither moth nor rust doth corrupt, and where

---

[25] Jim Newheiser, *Opening up Proverbs* (Leominster, England: Day One Publications, 2008), 126–27.

[26] To hoard does not necessarily mean to store up excessively. However, it sometimes carries the connotation of storing up in a "greedy or miserly or otherwise unreasonable manner." *Webster's Third New International Dictionary* (Springfield: G. and C. Merriam Company, 1961). The following treatment will use the term with its negative connotation.

thieves do not break through nor steal: for where your treasure is, there will your heart be also (Matt. 6:19–21).

Jesus says that one must, above all else, lay up treasure in heaven. Broadus correctly surmises that one lays up treasure in heaven by "doing and suffering for Christ's sake (Matt. 5:11–12, 44–46; 6:6; 2 Cor. 4:17), and among other things, by a right use of earthly possessions."[27] Jesus demands that a Christian use his possessions properly and not that he give them up entirely. He no more intended for the Christian to give away all of his money than He did for him to give away all his clothes.[28] The key point is that the Christian must not allow his storing up to hinder his devotion to God.

Furthermore, the Christian must not hoard by storing up selfishly. Jesus condemned selfish hoarding in His parable of the rich fool (Luke 12:16–21). Having enjoyed a bumper crop (v. 16), the rich man decided to hoard all of his surplus so that he could enjoy ease and comfort for years to come (vv. 18–19). We should note that his wealth seems to be God-given and honestly earned. However, his plans were interrupted by Him Who calls all men to account and at the time of His appointment. We learn that this man, who was following the natural order of business success, had one problem, and that was a spiritually fatal error. His mistake with eternal consequences was that while storing up treasure "for himself" (v. 21), he had neglected his spiritual life. The phrase "for himself" shows his self-centeredness and implies his lack of focus on godliness. The result of his self-focus and his main problem was that he was not "rich toward God." Though rich in earthly goods, he was utterly destitute of affection for and relationship with God.

---

[27] John A. Broadus, *Commentary on the Gospel of Matthew* (Valley Forge: Judson Press, 1886), 145.

[28] D. A. Carson, *The Sermon on the Mount* (Grand Rapids: Baker, 1978), 76–77.

Ultimately, because of their spiritual poverty, such men experience not the comforts of their wealth but the unending torment of separation from God. (Note the story of the rich man who neglected the needy Lazarus in Luke 16:23–25.) Bock's comments sum up Jesus' teaching: "Wealth toward self is poverty before God. The comfort that comes from wealth and the power derived from materialism provide only a fleeting and false security, a vain effort at control. . . . Wealth's only legacy is its fleeting nature (Luke 6:24–25)."[29] Only a fool would make fleeting wealth his heart's treasure.

RELIANCE ON WEALTH

Ironically, one of the dangers of successful financial planning is dependence upon wealth rather than upon God. The same Solomon who prayed for wisdom rather than riches fell away from God as his pleasures and affluence increased (1 Kings 11:1–10). The Bible repeatedly warns about man's propensity to trust his wealth instead of his God.

For example, Job said, "If I have made gold my hope, or have said to the fine gold, Thou art my confidence; . . . Let thistles grow instead of wheat, and cockle instead of barley" (31:24, 40). He admits that he could have made gold his confidence, but he also insists that he never had. Job foresaw the danger of making wealth his idol when his wealth became "great" (31:25). Solomon also recognized the danger of depending on accumulated wealth. He warned, "He that trusteth in his riches shall fall; but the righteous shall flourish as a branch" (Prov. 11:28). The antithesis in the verse classifies the man who trusts in wealth as unrighteous.[30] Because he is unrighteous, he is headed for a fall. This rich man goes a step beyond trusting his wealth instead of God; he even believes

---

[29] D. L. Bock, *Luke: Volume 2* in *Baker Exegetical Commentary on the New Testament* (Grand Rapids: Baker, 1996), 1155.

[30] Toy, 237.

that his riches will protect him from judgment.[31] He is misguided, however, and certain to experience a destructive fall. Indeed, he is headed for spiritual ruin.[32]

Recognizing the danger of trusting in wealth, Jeremiah pronounced God's judgment on doing so. In a prophetic oracle he foretold Moab's desolation and the reason for it: "Because of your trust in your own achievements and treasures, even you yourself will be captured; . . . The disaster of Moab will soon come, and his calamity has swiftly hastened" (48:7*a*, 16, NASB). Moab, like the rich man in Proverbs 11:28, trusted in riches as a protection from danger. But again, the writer declared that riches provide no shelter from God's wrath. In fact, reliance on riches is sometimes the very attitude that provokes God's wrath.

Quoting Jesus' words to His disciples, Mark also conveyed the danger of dependence on wealth: "Children, how hard is it for them that trust in riches to enter into the kingdom of God" (10:24*b*). These are astounding words, for they clearly imply the impossibility of salvation for the one relying on riches.[33] They also suggest that rich men have a tendency to rely on their wealth. Nevertheless, Jesus is condemning not wealth, but those who have trusted and are still trusting in it. Rich men too can enter God's kingdom, not because of their millions or billions, but rather in spite of their wealth. Like all others who will admit their spiritual poverty, they can be saved by grace through faith.[34]

---

[31] Ibid. Toy offers Prov. 10:2 and 11:4 in support of this idea. Ps. 49:6–7 also support the idea that some rich men believe their wealth will protect them.

[32] Several other references in Proverbs use the verb "to fall" to connote spiritual ruin or disaster (11:5; 22:14; 28:10, 14, 18).

[33] See the next verse (10:25), where Jesus likens the impossible task of the camel's going through the eye of a small sewing needle to that of a rich man's entering the kingdom of God.

[34] Joseph of Arimathea was a well-to-do follower of Christ (Matt. 27:57), as was Zacchaeus (Luke 19:1–9). Also, Simon Peter retained some of his property, for he owned a

Luke, too, quoted Jesus on the peril of reliance upon wealth. Climaxing His exhortation for followers to count the cost of discipleship, Jesus says, "So likewise, whosoever he be of you that forsaketh not all that he hath, he cannot be my disciple" (Luke 14:33). With this stricture, Jesus enjoins more an attitude than a practice. He does not necessarily intend for every disciple to sell all of his possessions, but He does demand that every disciple be willing to. True discipleship cannot coexist with an attitude of dependence on wealth.

A logical inference from the above references is that one who trusts in riches cannot begin to make proper financial plans. A genuine disinterestedness in the pursuit of riches is a prerequisite for legitimately Christian financial planning. When the Christian derives his sense of security from money rather than from God, he is already a victim of idolatry.[35] Therefore, a major caution in financial planning must be to avoid reliance on wealth.

How can one know if he is relying upon his wealth? Two texts help answer that question. The first is the response of the rich young ruler who came to Jesus with a genuine interest in salvation. Jesus told him that he lacked only selling his property and giving to the poor (Mark 10:21). The young man's response was that he became *sad* and *grieved* (10:22). Are you grieved at the thought of losing your wealth? If so, you are likely trusting in your wealth. The other text that helps us understand the right attitude toward wealth is Hebrews 10:34, which tells of persecuted Christians who "took joyfully the spoiling of their goods." Would you and I be able joyfully and by faith to give up our goods for Christ's sake as those early Christians did?

---

house in Capernaum (Luke 4:38).

[35] MacArthur, *Giving: God's Way*, 25.

PREOCCUPATION WITH FINANCIAL MATTERS

Financial planning in our day seems to be excessively complicated. Who really understands how the financial system works with all of its bonds, treasuries, hedge funds, derivatives, mutual funds, Roths, IRAs, and so on? But even in Christ's day, money matters often became complex, and people easily became preoccupied with them. The problem, however, is not the complexity of money matters, but the preoccupation with one's own financial issues. Being a good steward is one thing; being absorbed with money matters is another. Often such inordinate focus on money results from the love of money. This inordinate focus can also result from a lack of trust in God. Therefore, recognizing these problems, the Scripture writers addressed this subject of preoccupation with money matters.

For instance, Matthew records that Jesus taught His disciples, "Seek ye first the kingdom of God, and his righteousness; and all these things shall be added unto you. Take therefore no thought for the morrow: for the morrow shall take thought for the things of itself" (Matt. 6:33–34a). On the surface Jesus' words seem to prohibit financial planning. However, what Jesus censures is not provision of life's necessities, but seeking those necessities with an anxious, worried spirit.[36] Jesus also taught that the Christian must always give priority of time and effort to cultivating and practicing "personal righteousness."[37] Rather than becoming preoccupied with material pursuits, the believer must constantly subordinate them to the ambition to grow in grace.

As the previous reference suggested, preoccupation with financial affairs will bring anxiety. But even worse, such preoccupation can result in the forfeiture of one's life, spiritually and eternally.

---

[36] Broadus, 150.

[37] Ibid., 151.

Jesus' question form—"For what will it profit a man if he gains the whole world and forfeits his soul? Or what will a man give in exchange for his soul?" (Matt. 16:26, NASB)—required the hearer to answer with the admission that he could exchange no amount of wealth for his soul. All the money in the world could never buy a right standing with God. The danger of absorption in money matters could hardly be more vivid. To "forfeit one's soul" is eternally fatal, for it is to fail to "secure salvation."[38]

Jesus further illustrated the peril of preoccupation with financial matters when He explained, "The seed which fell among the thorns, these are the ones who have heard, and as they go on their way they are choked with worries and riches and pleasures of this life, and bring no fruit to maturity" (Luke 8:14, NASB). Riches can so dwarf the seedling of God's Word in the heart that it never produces "fruit 'for everlasting life'" (John 4:36).[39] In this context "riches" implies a preoccupation with the pursuit of wealth. Thus Jesus again demonstrates that preoccupation with financial matters can hinder one from securing salvation. This is a sobering passage, especially since the writer connected riches with the "pleasures" of this life as a threat to bearing spiritual fruit. We must not think of these as innocent pleasures if they are distracting the heart from the Word that has been sown. So how much energy and thought (worry?) are you giving to the pursuit of adding to your wealth and enjoying the comforts of the typical lifestyle? Based on this parable we see that the comparative amount of time and energy and thought one gives to knowing and internalizing the Word of God provides an accurate rule for assessing whether or not one is preoccupied with wealth.

---

[38] R. C. H. Lenski, *The Interpretation of St. Matthew's Gospel* (Minneapolis: Augsburg Publishing House, 1964), 646.

[39] William Hendriksen, *New Testament Commentary: Exposition of the Gospel According to Luke* (Grand Rapids: Baker, 1978), 428.

Paul also warned of the danger of over-involvement with financial matters in his words to the Christian minister. "No soldier in active service," the veteran apostle wrote to youthful Timothy, "entangles himself in the affairs of everyday life, so that he may please the one who enlisted him as a soldier" (2 Tim. 2:4, NASB). Paul's simile teaches that preoccupation with business pursuits will hinder Christian service. Once enlisted in God's service, the Christian must not become entangled in the monetary pursuits of life. Although those pursuits may well be necessary—Paul himself engaged in tent making—they must not occupy an inordinate amount of the Christian's time or energy.

James gives the last biblical warning against monetary preoccupation with a scathing rebuke of the rich (5:1–6). He accuses them with these words: "You have lived luxuriously on earth and led a life of wanton pleasure; you have fattened your hearts in a day of slaughter" (5:5, NASB). The rich of James's day were guilty of much more than a preoccupation with money. Nevertheless, their obsession with the luxuries and pleasures of life was part of their sin and thus serves as a caution against a fixation on having the latest technology, the shiniest car, the prettiest shoes, the greenest yard, the most comfortable furniture, the most spacious and updated kitchen, or the best meal at a choice restaurant. Like those given to overindulgence in food, such people are "fattening" themselves for the slaughter. Moo points out the contrast between their obsession with *earthly* comforts and the judgment coming upon them: "The easily overlooked phrase *on earth* contributes to these negative connotations, suggesting a contrast between the pleasures the rich have enjoyed in this world and the torment that awaits them in eternity."[40] These verses must be taken in the light of the

---

[40] D. J. Moo, *The Letter of James* in *The Pillar New Testament Commentary* (Grand Rapids; Eerdmans, 2000), 217.

full Scriptural teaching. We know from both the Scriptures and personal experience that some well-to-do Christians are generous and willing to share their wealth. However, the indisputable point is that they are a small minority, the exceptions to the rule.

In conclusion, the Christian may have only one preoccupation in life, and that is to "please him who hath chosen him to be a soldier" (2 Tim. 2:4*b*). Therefore, while fulfilling his responsibility of financial planning, the Christian must limit the time, thought, and energy that he devotes to money matters. He must carefully maintain his spiritual priorities. A financial adviser has wisely concluded that "if business involvement requires that you sacrifice God's work or your family, it is *not* according to His plan."[41] The Psalmist adds that "it is vain" to be overburdened with monetary pursuits, "for He gives to His beloved even in his sleep" (127:2, NASB).

IMPROPER ADVICE

For the Christian to get advice from the ungodly is spiritually dangerous. This does not mean that the advice of the non-Christian is necessarily bad, for he may have good information and counsel about financial matters. Anyone who can understand math can understand economics to some degree. Without doubt, many non-Christian businessmen operate on the basis of biblically sound financial principles because of the good results. Nevertheless, the Christian must guard against blindly following the advice of such men, for characteristically they neither understand nor adhere to biblical truth.[42]

Concerning the matter of the ungodly's advice, the Psalmist exclaimed, "Blessed is the man that walketh not in the counsel of

---

[41] Burkett, *Your Finances*, 94.

[42] See 1 Cor. 2:14.

the ungodly, nor standeth in the way of sinners, nor sitteth in the seat of the scornful" (Ps. 1:1). "Bliss" comes to the man who avoids the companionship and advice of those who are morally lax and unstable of character.[43] The counsel of the unsaved will likely misguide the Christian. Therefore, he must instead allow the Lord's "counsel" (Ps. 73:24) to guide him. The man seeking God's blessing upon his financial plans should secure advice primarily from God by constantly delighting in and meditating on His Word (Ps. 1:2). He should take fiscal advice from the unsaved only as supplemental. Many godly men and women offer sound, biblical advice through books, websites, and seminars. The test of their validity will always be their adherence to biblical principles.

An example of the counsel of the ungodly that leads astray is simply that of much of the advertising business. If one were to follow the advice of the advertisements he sees and hears in one week, he would likely be hopelessly in debt for the rest of his life. See the chapter on indebtedness to get some examples of the financial advice of the ungodly and where that advice has led America.

INORDINATE INSURANCE CONCERN

A Christian can easily "go overboard" in attempting to insure himself and his family against calamities. There is nothing inherently wrong with buying insurance to preclude financial disaster. Insurance is wise in many instances. For example, health insurance is often wise. As one writer on Christian stewardship has said, "With rocketing costs for medical care . . . it would seem part of Christian responsibility for a family to try to maintain some kind of valuable health insurance policy, in order to protect itself from

---

[43] *TWOT*, 1:182, defines the masculine plural construct of אֶשֶׁר as "bliss"; *KD, Psalms*, 1:84.

complete financial shipwreck in case of serious illness."[44] Note that Crawford wrote over 40 years ago! How much more is that advice appropriate today, when a hospital stay of only a few hours can cost thousands of dollars? (Have you been to an emergency room lately?) Likewise, a homeowner's policy and car insurance are probably necessities in the modern world. But although insurance may be good Christian responsibility, the Christian must never use it as a panacea.

Fear of the future, an improper attitude for the Christian, often precipitates over-reliance on insurance. Because some Christians waver in their faith to trust God for needs, they become obsessed with protecting themselves. God has told the Christian to provide for his family, but not to protect it from every calamity. The believer must realize that insuring for every contingency is not only foolish, but impossible. Moreover, one must never forget that God often uses calamity to draw Christians closer to Himself. Those who experience unexpected trouble have God's invitation and promise: "Offer unto God thanksgiving; and pay thy vows unto the most High: and call upon me in the day of trouble: I will deliver thee, and thou shalt glorify me" (Ps. 50:14–15).

CONCLUSION

The Christian has several responsibilities pertaining to financial planning. A bulleted list will remind us of those duties and help us visualize them.

- Providing for children and for other family members

- Investing money wisely

- Storing up for lean times

---

[44] John R. Crawford, *A Christian and His Money* (Nashville: Abingdon Press, 1967), 89.

- Avoiding
  - Foolish spending
  - Get-rich-quick schemes
  - Hoarding
  - Reliance on wealth
  - Preoccupation with financial matters
  - Improper advice
  - Attempting to insure for every contingency

Of course, every Christian can claim such blessed promises as "The Lord is my shepherd; I shall not want" (Ps. 23:1), "The young lions do lack, and suffer hunger: but they that seek the Lord shall not want any good thing" (Ps. 34:10), "But seek ye first the kingdom of God, and his righteousness; and all these things shall be added unto you" (Matt. 6:33), and "My God shall supply all your need according to his riches in glory by Christ Jesus" (Phil. 4:19). However, these promises no more mitigate the responsibility of financial planning than the security of possessing everlasting life mitigates the responsibility to grow in holiness (2 Cor. 7:1).

Because financial planning is a Christian duty, the Christian must determine how to fulfill the obligation in his particular circumstances. Throughout this chapter the specifics of financial planning—how much to set aside for children and relatives, how much to save, how much to invest, and how much insurance to acquire—have been conspicuously absent, and for good reason. No one can dictate the particulars of financial planning, because the Lord has purposefully given the principles of this planning in general terms. Just as no one can tell the Christian how much to give, so no one can tell him how much to save or invest. This does not mean that financial advisers err in offering guidelines for a Christian's financial planning. There are certain money matters in today's economy to which every adult Christian should give attention.

A budget and an up-to-date will are two musts for the Christian's financial planning. Of course, there are many other aspects of financial planning that may well be God's will for the individual Christian. The advantages and disadvantages of these aspects are beyond the scope of this chapter. Almost every large Christian institution employs a financial adviser specifically for helping Christians make plans to benefit the Lord's work. The Christian should avail himself of such advice. By carefully weighing godly counsel, by studying God's Word, and by prayer, the Christian must and can make proper financial plans. No one can determine for the Christian exactly what plans he should make. The Lord directs some Christians, such as George Müller, to save no money at all, but He directs others to save, to insure, and to invest.[45] The conclusion of the whole matter might be stated in beatitude form: "Blessed is the man who has his financial affairs in order."

---

[45] See footnote 1 in Chapter 1 concerning Müller's attitude toward saving.

3

GUIDELINES FOR CHRISTIAN GIVING

Although many emphasize the biblical principle of tithing for Christian giving, the Scriptural emphasis is actually much broader. Because believers need to know God's emphases in this most important matter, this chapter will look at a broad range of biblical data. Knowing many of the details will enable us to paint the big picture of how God wants us to give for the furtherance of His kingdom and purposes.

ABOUT TITHING

As already suggested, tithing gets much attention, and, even apart from its biblical moorings, the concept has some practical arguments in its favor. For example, tithing is good because it provides a specific plan for giving. Moreover, tithing is beneficial because it encourages discipline. Also, tithing reminds the giver that the Lord's work and the Lord's workers deserve more than the tidbits they often receive. That tithing often fosters liberality is another argument in its favor. Finally, tithing is commendable because it has brought spiritual joy to many believers.[1] However, although these practical arguments have merit, the same arguments could be used to suggest that the Christian should give 11 percent, or 12 percent, or some other percentage. Therefore, the only compelling arguments for determining the amount or percentage of Christian giving are those based on solid biblical exegesis.

---

[1] Marvin E. Tate, "Tithing: Legalism or Benchmark?" *Review and Expositor*, LXX (Spring, 1973), 161.

The Scriptures offer solid evidence for tithing in the examples of Abraham and Jacob. Both of these men may have tithed: Abraham tithed for sure, and Jacob promised to tithe. But more importantly, they both tithed before Moses gave the tithing requirements of the Law. Therefore, tithing is more than legislation; it is a principle. When Abraham learned that a confederacy of four northern kings had looted Sodom and had taken Lot and his family captive, he and his company, in loyalty to Lot, pursued and defeated the kings. He also brought back Lot and all that belonged to him (Gen. 14:8–16). On the return home, Abraham met Melchizedek and voluntarily gave him a tenth of the victory spoils (Gen. 14:18–20). That Abraham gave a tenth, and not some other percentage, suggests that tithing was a well-known practice of his day. However, that Abraham regularly tithed cannot be proved. Genesis 14:20 and its parallel in Hebrews 7:1–9 provide the only biblical record that Abraham tithed. In this one instance Abraham did not tithe from all that he owned, but simply from the spoils of his victory. Therefore, a statement such as "Abraham *established* [emphasis added] an excellent system known as tithing"[2] overstates the data. Ross's assessment is more accurate: "This is not a normal tithing practice. Abram actually was tithing out of the spoils of war, things that formerly did not belong to him. It is still an act of submission and worship but not a sample of regular giving."[3]

Jacob's mention of tithing, however, provides supplemental information that may validate the perpetuity of tithing. On his way from Beersheba to Haran, Jacob spent a night in Luz, which he later renamed Bethel. The next morning Jacob voluntarily vowed to God that he would tithe all that God gave him in return for

---

[2] G. Thornton Hall, "Stewardship" (Hampton, VA: Central Baptist Church, n.d.), 6. (Mimeographed).

[3] Allen Ross, *Recalling the Hope of Glory* (Grand Rapids: Kregel, 2006), 149.

divine protection and favor (Gen. 28:20–22). Jacob clearly believed that tithing was a pious practice.

Several conclusions arise from these two examples of pre-Mosaic tithing. First, tithing was a voluntary practice. Nowhere does the biblical record state that God commanded either Abraham or Jacob to tithe.[4] They tithed willingly. In the second place, Abraham's tithing pleased God.[5] Since Scripture favorably cites his example of tithing, and since the episode with Melchizedek has the aura of genuine worship about it, a valid conclusion is that Abraham's giving was an act of worship, pleasing to God. Finally, Christ's death and perfect sacrifice, although abolishing certain aspects of the Mosaic Law (Col. 2:13–17), did not abolish the principle or spirit of tithing as far as we can discern. Allen Ross rightly observes, "What the law revealed about the will of God is still binding for instruction in righteousness (2 Tim. 3:16), that is the spirit of the law remains; so giving, and giving generously, to the Lord and to the needy, is part of spiritual devotion and worship."[6] God took delight in voluntary tithing several hundred years before Moses was even born. Therefore, we may conclude that tithing is still an acceptable practice. However, as will be seen, the biblical emphasis is not on tithing, but on giving cheerfully, liberally, and proportionately.

---

[4] The giving of a tenth to a deity was widespread in ancient times. Tate (153) reports that tithing was "practiced in such diverse lands and cultures as Babylonia, Egypt, Persia, Greece, Rome, Phoenicia, Lydia, Syria, Carthage, China, and among Mohammedans generally." However, Abraham did not necessarily learn tithing from a heathen culture. He actually pre-dates most of the heathen cultures listed. God could have revealed tithing to Abraham and to Jacob in some way other than written form. John R. Rice makes much of this possibility. See *All About Christian Giving* (Wheaton: Sword of the Lord Publishers, 1954), 22–23.

[5] No doubt Jacob also would have pleased God with his tithes. However, the biblical evidence provides no record that Jacob was true to his vow. But considering Jacob's growth in spiritual maturity over the years, it is likely that he eventually tithed.

[6] Ross, 207.

Moses' Commands

John R. Rice deduced in one of his chapter titles that "The Old Testament Teaches Christians to Tithe." One basis for his deduction is that "All Israel under Mosaic Law Was Required to Tithe."[7] In spite of the sincere conviction of men such as Rice, this argument is weak for several reasons. In the first place, it does not give an accurate definition of Mosaic tithing. Moses commanded the Israelites to give not one, but two, and possibly even three tithes. The first instruction concerning the tithe was,

> And all the tithe of the land, whether of the seed of the land, or of the fruit of the tree, is the Lord's: it is holy unto the Lord. . . . And concerning the tithe of the herd, or of the flock, even of whatsoever passeth under the rod, the tenth shall be holy unto the Lord (Lev. 27:30, 32).

This legislation required a tithe of the seed-harvest yield, of the fruit of the tree, and of the cattle or sheep.[8] The tither could redeem the tenth of the grain or of the fruit by buying it at 120 percent of its market value (v. 31). However, the tither could not redeem his tithe of cattle or of sheep. He was required to give every tenth animal that passed under his rod.[9] Even if the designated animal was especially strong or especially weak, the tither had no choice but to give it (vv. 32–33).[10]

Moses further legislated concerning this tithe that the Levites were to receive it as their means of support. Then, they themselves were to give a tenth of the people's tithe for the support of the high priest (Num. 18:21–28; cf. Neh. 10:38). A major element of this

---

[7] Rice, 23.

[8] Cf. Deut. 14:22–23 and 2 Chron. 31:5–6.

[9] The herds and flocks were counted as they passed out to pasture (cf. Ezek. 20:37 and Jer. 33:13).

[10] If a man vowed to give an animal to the Lord, and then exchanged a poorer one, both the original animal and the substitute were to be "holy," that is, dedicated and given to the Lord (Lev. 27:10).

tithing, by both the people and the priest, was its compulsory aspect. It was law. The people owed this tenth to the Lord; it *belonged* to Him (Lev. 27:26, 30).

But more than a tenth belonged to the Lord, for Moses prescribed a second tithe in Deuteronomy 12:5–18.[11] This tithe was to be brought to the central place of worship (vv. 5, 11, 14, 18) and used there as a sacred meal for the offerer's family and the Levites within his town.[12] This yearly festival promoted joy and fellowship among the Israelites. Every year the Israelite was to take this second tithe from the harvest yield of the seed he had sown (Deut. 14:22). If the distance to the central worship place was great, the offerer could exchange his tithe of produce for money and bring that money to the place of worship (14:24–25). Once there, he could buy whatever he desired for the festal meal (14:26). This liberty of disposal differentiates the second tithe from the first. The purpose for this tithe, to provide for the yearly feast, also differentiates it from the first tithe, which provided support for the Levites only.

Moses concluded his instruction concerning tithes in Deuteronomy 14:28–29 and 26:12–14. Every third year, designated the "year of the tithe," the tithe was to be distributed among "the

---

[11] Not all scholars agree that Moses required two tithes from the same people. Charles L. Feinberg claims that Moses prescribed different practices as the times and places changed. "Tithe," *ZPEB* (1976), 5:757. Similarly, S. R. Driver dogmatically asserts that "the two laws, it is impossible to doubt, speak of one and the same tithe; and the discrepancy between them arises simply from the fact that they represent different stages in the history of the institution." *A Critical and Exegetical Commentary on Deuteronomy* (New York: Charles Scribner's Sons, 1916), 171. However, Driver's solution to the differences between the tithe requirements is not satisfactory because he bases it on a late date (seventh century B.C. [p. xliv ff.]) for Deuteronomy. This late date cannot be correct. The inspired record states that Moses wrote Deuteronomy in the fortieth year and the eleventh month from the time of the Exodus (Deut. 1:3; 31:22). Moreover, Moses wrote Leviticus and part of Numbers near the beginning of the wilderness wandering (Num. 1:1) and the rest of Numbers and Deuteronomy near the end of the wilderness wandering (Num. 35:1; 36:13; Deut. 1:1; 31:22). Therefore, the regulations concerning the two tithes could not have been given more than forty years apart.

[12] *KD, Pentateuch*, 3:356.

Levite, the stranger, the fatherless, and the widow" (26:12). Possibly this tithe was simply the second festival tithe with a special triennial use for the underprivileged. However, this could also have been a third and separate tithe. Of the two views, the idea of a third tithe seems more likely. Although three tithes sound excessively burdensome, both the biblical data and important non-canonical witnesses favor the idea. The Hebrew text gives no hint that the festival tithe (second) and the poor tithe (third) were the same, except with a different application every third year.[13] The argument for only two tithes says that on every third year the Israelite was not to follow the regular procedure of taking the second, festival tithe to the central worship place, but rather was to distribute it among the needy at home.[14] However, Moses does not offer a triennial exemption from the festival tithe. Several times he commands every male to participate in the yearly festivals, and he makes no exception for the third year.

Three extra-biblical witnesses further indicate that Moses prescribed three separate tithes. The first witness, the author of the apocryphal book of Tobit, proudly explains his fidelity to truth and the practice of righteousness:

> But I alone went often to Jerusalem at the feasts, as it was ordained unto all the people of Israel by an everlasting decree, having the first fruits and tenths of increase, with that which was first shorn; and them gave I at the altar to the priests the children of Aaron. The first tenth part of all increase I gave to the sons of Aaron, who ministered at Jerusalem: and the third I gave unto them to whom it was

---

[13] However, the Septuagint does indicate that they are the same. It designates the tithe for the poor as the second tithe (τὸ δεύτερον ἐπιδέκατον).

[14] See Eugene Merrill's comments in *Deuteronomy*, Cornerstone Biblical Commentary (Carol Stream, IL: Tyndale House, 2008), 620.

meet, as Deborah my father's mother had commanded me, because I was left an orphan by my father.[15]

Plainly, Tobit thought it his duty to give three tithes. Similarly, Josephus bears witness to the idea of three tithes:

> Besides those two tithes which I have already said you are to pay every year, the one for the Levites, the other for the festivals, you are to bring every third year a tithe to be distributed to those that want; to women also that are widows, and to children that are orphans.[16]

Finally, Jerome too understood that Moses prescribed one tenth for the Levites, another tenth for festival purposes, and a third tenth for the poor.[17] Therefore, the testimony is strong in favor of three separate tithes.[18] However, determining whether Moses called for two tithes or for three is not essential to prove that Moses prescribed a total of more than 10 percent for the Israelites. He definitely prescribed at least 20 percent. Therefore, those who preach that Christians should tithe because Moses commanded the Israelites to tithe, should instead preach that Christians ought to give two tithes (20 percent), or even three tithes every third year (for a 23.3 percent yearly average). Actually, the giving requirements that Moses enjoined upon the Israelites went considerably beyond even the three tithes. A summary of the faithful Israelite's giving obligations would include these obligations: portions from several kinds of sacrifices and offerings, the first fruits of the land, proceeds of

---

[15] Tobit 1:6–8.

[16] William Whiston, trans., *Josephus: Complete Works* (Grand Rapids: Kregel Publications, 1960), 98.

[17] *Commentary on Ezekiel* xlv, 1:565, cited in "Tithe," *M'Clintock and Strong's Cyclopedia of Biblical, Theological, and Ecclesiastical Literature* (1867; repr., 1970), 10:432.

[18] Mark Rooker states matter-of-factly, "There were three tithes for the ancient Israelites: (1) the general tithe (Lev. 27), (2) the tithe of the sacred meal with the Levite (Deut. 14:22–27), and (3) the tithe paid every three years to the poor (Deut. 14:28–29)." *Leviticus*, vol. 3A, *The New American Commentary* (Nashville: Broadman, 2000), 328.

sheep-shearing, the tithes, and wood for the altar fire.[19] "Perhaps, therefore, we are justified in supposing that the Mosaic Law required the Israelite to set apart, in some way or other connected with his religion, from one-fourth to a third of his income."[20]

In summary, Moses indeed commanded tithing, but he also commanded much more. In order to fulfill the Mosaic requirements, a dutiful Israelite had to give more than 20 percent of his total income. Summarizing the data, Allen Ross states that "a faithful Israelite family could pay anywhere between 22 and 30 percent in a given year."[21] Thus the argument that Christians should tithe because Moses commanded tithing is misleading and even faulty. To be more accurate, the argument should be, "Christians should give more than 20 percent because Moses commanded the Israelites to give more than 20 percent." However, a further consideration puts even this restatement of the argument in a new perspective.

Requiring Christians to give as the Israelites did under Moses draws a faulty parallel. During the time of Moses, the Israelites lived under a theocratic government. But Christians today live under various forms of democratic, socialistic, and communistic government. Much of a Jew's giving before the monarchy went to support the government of his nation, a government that the priests superintended. Living in a theocracy, the Israelite did not need to distinguish between giving to the Lord's work and paying taxes. In fact, he could not make the distinction, because religion permeated his society and its government. Therefore, one cannot draw a strict parallel between Jewish and Christian giving unless one either allows the paying of taxes as part of Christian giving or

---

[19] Bruce Corley, "The Intertestamental Perspective of Stewardship," *Southwestern Journal of Theology*, XIII (Spring 1971), 23.

[20] Henry Landsdell, *The Sacred Tenth*, 2 vols. (Grand Rapids: Baker, 1955), 1:76–77.

[21] Ross, 206.

differentiates paying taxes and giving in the Mosaic economy.[22] Probably no one would accept the former alternative, and the latter alternative is an exegetical impossibility. Such a dichotomy of giving did not exist under the theocracy. One must conclude that no strict parallel can be drawn between giving in a theocracy and giving under a non-theocratic government. Ross acknowledges the differences between then and now:

> It was all necessary because the laws were part of a full socio-economic system, not just the support of a religious organization—although that would be no small task since the Levites who were to be supported were one-twelfth of the nation. This is why it is not easy to transfer the rules of tithes and offerings over to the church—a simple 10 percent is a small part of what Israelites paid.[23]

In analyzing the Mosaic requirements, we must also note that Moses exempted the poor from some requirements. Some men have failed to recognize this exemption. For example, the sentiment of one pastor is, "Everybody ought to tithe. I mean everybody."[24] Similarly, evangelist John R. Rice penned his conviction that "there is not a hint in the Bible that the poor were to be exempted from the tithe."[25] However, one may legitimately infer from biblical data that Moses did indeed exempt the poor from at least one of the tithes. Of the three tithes that Moses commanded, one was especially for the poor.[26] That the poor were to contribute this

---

[22] Dale A. Brueggemann explains that in effect these giving regulations became a tax. "After captivity, the tithe became a Temple tax (Neh. 10:38; 13:5, 10). Actually it has that tone in this text (18:21), but under a monarchy, this could quickly degenerate into a royal tax (1 Sam. 8:17)." *Numbers*, Cornerstone Bible Commentary (Carol Stream, IL: Tyndale House, 2008), 334.

[23] Ross, 207.

[24] Tom Malone, "Tithes of All," *The Baptist Vision* (September 1, 1976), 2.

[25] Rice, 141.

[26] See the preceding discussion of Deut. 14:28–29 and 26:12–14. The triennial tithe was especially for the poor.

tithe for their own support is hardly conceivable. The text states that the Levite and the underprivileged—the stranger, the fatherless, and the widow—were to come and eat and be satisfied (Deut. 14:29), but it mentions nothing about their bringing a tithe. The plain implication is that the Levites and the poor were to enjoy the tithes of others whom God had prospered.

To review, the teaching about God's giving requirements under the Mosaic Law yields three major points. First, Moses commanded the Israelites to give not one, but two and possibly three tithes. Second, the Jews were giving under a theocracy, and such giving was similar to paying taxes to support the system of government. Finally, we learn that Moses exempted the poor from giving one of the tithes. Therefore, because Moses' regulations did not apply to all alike, making tithing incumbent on all Christians alike is an improper generalizing of the biblical commands. On the other hand, we should seriously think of the implications of the Mosaic requirements regarding our giving. A logical application would be to note that the Lord's stipulations provided for (1) the Lord's work (the temple system), (2) the joyful, extended fellowship of the Lord's people and (3) the needy, and to ask if our giving sufficiently takes into account the support of those areas. Gene Getz makes this observation about the Jewish giving: "From a pragmatic point of view, one thing is crystal clear. If all Christians gave the same regular amounts to the church as the Jews gave to maintain their religious system, there would never be unmet economic needs in the ministry today."[27]

JESUS' COMMENDATIONS

"Woe unto you, Pharisees! for ye tithe mint and rue and all manner of herbs, and pass over judgment and the love of God: these ought

---

[27] Gene Getz, *A Biblical Theology of Material Possessions* (Chicago: Moody, 1990), 210.

ye to have done, and not to leave the other undone" (Luke 11:42; cf. Matt. 23:23 and Luke 18:12). Sometimes these words are construed as a commendation of tithing and then adduced as proof that Christians should tithe. Obviously, Jesus did acknowledge that the scrupulous tithing of the Pharisees was obligatory for them. However, this is not a valid proof-text for making tithing incumbent upon Christians.

Although Jesus commended the Pharisees for obeying the tithing requirements of the law, it does not follow that Christians should tithe as the Pharisees did. As the avowed champions of Judaism, the Pharisees "ought" to have obeyed the Mosaic requirements for giving, and thus they "ought" to have tithed. But Christians are not adherents of Judaism, many of whose "ordinances" Christ's cross and resurrection abolished.[28] Christ did commend the Pharisees for tithing, but tithing by any group other than the Pharisees is not mentioned again in the New Testament, except for the example of Abraham and the Levites (Heb. 7:2–9). The paucity of evidence can go either way, as Gary Reimers has pointed out: "Rather than point to the absence of a verse that confirms the tithe during the church era, perhaps we should notice the absence of a verse that withdraws it from the category of God's expectations."[29] However, the lack of evidence also suggests that Christians are not *necessarily* required to tithe as the Jews were. The primary application of Luke 11:42 for the Christian is not that he should tithe, but that he should give priority to fulfilling the ethical requirements of the law.[30]

---

[28] Col. 2:13–15. See R. C. H. Lenski's discussion of the Christian's relationship to the law of tithing. *The Interpretation of St. Luke's Gospel* (Minneapolis: Augsburg Publishing House, 1961), 661.

[29] Gary Reimers, *The Glory Due His Name* (Greenville, SC: Bob Jones University Press, 2009), 40.

[30] The context is that of denunciation of Pharisaic religiosity. Christ was not suggesting a system of Christian giving; He was rebuking misguided and hypocritical zeal. He

PAUL'S GIVING INSTRUCTIONS

Paul's writings take us to the next period in the growth of God's kingdom and in particular to the founding of New Testament churches. Those churches had financial needs and thus were in need of instruction regarding giving. The giving instructions in Paul's writings then provide further help in understanding tithing.

1 Corinthians 16:2

1 Corinthians 16:2 is often used as a proof text for giving and even for tithing. However, though the text provides a window into New Testament giving practices, it cannot be used to legitimate tithing. In fact, a careful analysis of Paul's words in 1 Corinthians 16:2 invalidates the argument that Paul taught tithing here. Furthermore, a survey of Paul's instructions about giving proves that Paul's emphases lay elsewhere.

"The principle of tithing," affirms one preacher, "is clearly taught in the New Testament."[31] As proof for his position he adduces 1 Corinthians 16:2, "Upon the first day of the week let every one of you lay by him in store, as God hath prospered him, that there be no gatherings when I come," with the following applications:

> This kind of giving would be *proportionate.* "As God hath prospered him" The tithe is the proportion of each. . . .

> This kind of giving would be *practical.* "That there be no gatherings when I come." Tithing finances God's work.[32]

John R. Rice likewise claims that 1 Corinthians 16:2 teaches Christian tithing. His reasoning is better and worthy of consideration:

> It is obvious that the church at Corinth started with converted Jews. . . . Now what proportion would Jews suppose

---

was emphasizing the "relative insignificance of careful tithing when compared with the deeper requirements of the Torah." Tate, 159.

[31] Norman H. Wells, "Tithing," *Central Contender*, 26 May 1967, 3.

[32] Ibid.

they should lay aside for the Lord? The answer is obvious. These Jews, all their lives had been giving tithes and offerings for the Levitical priesthood at Jerusalem. When they were converted, and Paul said, "Let every one of you lay by him in store, as God hath prospered him," they would naturally suppose they should lay aside tithes. And Paul himself, a Jew and accustomed all his life to bringing tithes, would have that in mind. No other proportion is ever mentioned in the Bible as a proper minimum and yardstick for giving of means to God![33]

Dr. Rice's reasons sound plausible, for Paul was a Jew, and many of the Corinthian converts were Jews. However, two factors make it unlikely that Paul was commanding tithing.

The first problem with assuming that Paul commanded tithing is Paul's absolute silence on tithing. Dr. Rice asserts that Paul would have had tithing in mind, but if he did, the question arises as to why he did not mention it. Paul could easily have exhorted the Corinthians to tithe. But instead, he simply told them to give in proportion to their means, as God had blessed them materially. Certainly Paul's failure to mention tithing is just as instructive as the Jewish background of him and his readers. A further problem with assuming that Paul had tithing in mind is the very phraseology he used. His exhortation, "each one of you is to put aside and save, as he may prosper" (NASB), does not admit of tithing. The apparent meaning is that each Corinthian believer was to give proportionately.[34] However, the proportion was not necessarily the

---

[33] Rice, 32.

[34] David Garland observes that "Paul is not soliciting a tithe but is asking all to give as they are able (cf. 2 Cor. 8:11–12). . . . Paul asks them to give out of their abundance, not sacrificially (contrast the giving of the Macedonians in 2 Cor. 8:2–3). It might be less than a tithe; it might be far more than a tithe." *1 Corinthians* in *Baker Exegetical Commentary on the New Testament* (Grand Rapids: Baker, 2003), 754.

same for all; each was to give in proportion to his means.[35] None were exempt ("let *every one* of you)" but the proportion for each was not specified and not even expected to be the same each week, for one's prospering might vary with time. Paul had no apparent concern that they tithe; rather, his concern was that they all give and that they give in proportion to God's measure of blessing. Another factor militating against making this verse a call for systematic tithing is that Paul was collecting a special offering from these Gentiles for the poor saints in Jerusalem (Rom. 15:25–27) and not laying down guidelines for regular church offerings.

One would expect Paul at least to mention tithing if he considered it an imperative aspect of Christian giving. Paul was concerned about money, not so much for himself, but for those in need. He spent much of his third missionary journey superintending a collection from newly planted churches for the relief of the straitened brethren of the Jerusalem community (Acts 18:23–21:16; see especially Rom. 15:25–28 and 2 Cor. 8–9). Paul was concerned about monetary needs, and he gave many instructions for Christian giving. A survey of these instructions will provide a basis for us to establish principles for Christian giving.

1 Corinthians 9:7–14

Here Paul reasoned that Christians should financially support those who minister to their spiritual needs (see also Rom. 15:26–27; Gal. 6:6; and 1 Tim. 5:17–18). As proof for his argument, Paul cited Deuteronomy 25:4, "Thou shalt not muzzle the ox when he treadeth out the corn."[36] To refuse food to the laboring ox is inhumane. If God requires the rewarding of the dumb ox, which

---

[35] Charles Hodge, *An Exposition of the First Epistle to the Corinthians* (repr., Grand Rapids: Eerdmans, 1974), 363–64.

[36] Cf. 1 Tim. 5:18, where Paul quotes this passage and then encapsulates the teaching of Christ in the common proverb, "The labourer is worthy of his reward."

expends its energies for the good of many, He much more requires that His ministers, who are rational creatures, receive ample remuneration.[37] Not only does God require that the minister receive sufficient compensation, but the natural law of sowing and harvesting also demands it. The minister who sows spiritual things has the right to share in the material proceeds of the harvest (vv. 11–12*a*). If the benefits that he bestows are spiritual and therefore of infinite value, then it is a relatively small matter that he derive from his hearers things necessary for the support of the body.[38] Furthermore, in all religions, but especially in the Jewish religion, the principle holds true that those who minister in the temple legitimately derive their support from portions of temple sacrifices and offerings (v. 13). So God has directed that Christian ministers likewise draw their support from their constituency and not from secular employment (v. 14).[39]

1 Corinthians 13:3

"And though I bestow all my goods to feed the poor, . . . and have not charity, it profiteth me nothing." Giving, says Paul, benefits a Christian not at all if he does not actuate and accompany it with love. God wants the heart, and if He does not have that, neither tithing, nor, as the text says, giving 100 percent of one's goods, avails anything.[40] Man tends to think that "external acts of beneficence" are, in themselves, pleasing to God.[41] But God accords no value to external acts of religion alone. Perhaps this tendency to

---

[37] Hodge, *First Epistle to the Corinthians*, 157–58.

[38] Ibid., 159.

[39] Paul did not always follow this rule, however. He refused to take support from the Corinthians because he did not want to burden them (2 Cor. 11:7–9).

[40] Cf. Rom. 15:26–27; 2 Cor. 11:7–9. The one-time action contemplated is that in which one sells all that he possesses and gives the proceeds away. Leon Morris, *The First Epistle of Paul to the Corinthians* (Grand Rapids: Eerdmans, 1967), 183.

[41] Hodge, *First Epistle to the Corinthians*, 268.

overvalue outward religious performance is Paul's reason for never mentioning tithing, which can easily become an outward deed only.

2 Corinthians 8

In this, one of Paul's two outstanding chapters on Christian giving, he explained in detail how the Christian should give.[42] First, by implication, Christians should give liberally (v. 2). Even those who are poor, like the Macedonian Christians, may give generously.[43] Paul might have expected them to give according to their limited means, but they did even better and gave "beyond their power" (v. 3). Of course, Paul did not expect such sacrificial giving of everyone, for the general principle is to give according to what one has and not according to what one does not have (v. 12). But before one gives anything, he should first have "a willing mind" ("readiness," NASB). Thus Christians are not to give according to strict rules, but willingly and according to their ability. Again, Paul seemingly ignored tithing. That Paul had tithing in mind is highly unlikely. The clause "their deep poverty abounded unto the riches of their liberality" (v. 2) may well indicate that they gave far beyond 10 percent. Moreover, the principle of giving according to one's resources is not at all suggestive of tithing. If anything, it suggests that each Christian should determine for himself what proportion to give. Tasker is right in insisting that "once the readiness to give is there (and if it is not, no giving is of any value at all), the only further point to be decided is the amount; and this

---

[42] The other outstanding chapter is 2 Cor. 9. See the subsequent discussion for its treatment.

[43] Paul explains their situation as one of extreme poverty. "Their deep poverty" (ἡ κατὰ βάθους πτωχεία αὐτῶν) Philip E. Hughes explains as "their rock-bottom poverty." *Paul's Second Epistle to the Corinthians* (Grand Rapids: Eerdmans, 1962), 288.

depends on one consideration only, the financial resources of the donor."[44]

2 Corinthians 9

This chapter continues Paul's skillfully designed exhortation to the Corinthians to continue the collection they had begun. Verses six and seven represent a synopsis of Paul's teaching about Christian giving:

> Now this I say, he who sows sparingly will also reap sparingly; and he who sows bountifully will also reap bountifully. Each one must do just as he has purposed in his heart; not grudgingly or under compulsion; for God loves a cheerful giver (NASB).[45]

Several aspects of giving can be gleaned from these verses. As noted above, Christians should give liberally. A fundamental principle of giving is that "the liberal soul shall be made fat: and he that watereth shall be watered also himself" (Prov. 11:25). Further proving that liberal giving pleases God are these verses: "He that hath pity upon the poor lendeth unto the Lord; and that which he hath given will he pay him again" (Prov. 19:17), and, "with the same measure that ye mete withal it shall be measured to you again" (Luke 6:38b). In other words, giving is like the sowing of seed by the farmer, for, contrary to all appearances, both giving and sowing yield an abundant increase.[46] The more a Christian gives from a proper motivation, the more God showers blessings upon him in return.[47]

---

[44] Tasker, *The Second Epistle of Paul to the Corinthians*, 117.

[45] See Gal. 6:7–8 for a reiteration of the concept of reaping in proportion to sowing.

[46] Hughes, 329.

[47] The phrase literally reads, "He who is sowing with blessings shall also reap with blessings" (9:6b). God returns material and spiritual blessings to the one who gives freely and spontaneously.

Another aspect of Christian giving is that each Christian should give "according to the free choice of his heart" (9:7a).[48] Words could not be plainer; every Christian must decide in his own heart how much he should give. Some Christians may decide to give 10 percent, others may decide to give 20 percent, and still others 50 percent or more. Paul here requires no definite percentage. In fact, requiring a definite percentage might have hindered instead of encouraged liberal giving. By omitting any reference to a percentage, Paul makes it impossible for a Christian to be satisfied just because he has met the minimum standard of 10 percent.

That giving should be cheerful, rather than grudging or compulsory, is the final aspect of Paul's teaching.[49] One must not give and then wish to have the gift back. That is, a Christian must not give "out of sorrow" at the thought of parting with his money.[50] Neither should the Christian give because compelled to give in a variety of ways: high-pressure appeals, appeals by figures of authority, and public opinion.[51] According to Paul, compulsion is never a proper motivation for giving. The only proper motivation is love for God, which manifests itself by a willing and cheerful spirit of giving.

Since giving should not be compulsory, it must be thoughtful. Rather than allow himself to be swayed immediately by appeals calculated to stir his heart and to release his purse strings, the Christian should take enough time to discern thoughtfully

---

[48] Translation by W. J. Conybeare and J. S. Howson, *The Life and Epistles of St. Paul* (repr., Grand Rapids: Eerdmans, 1978), 455–56.

[49] The adjective "cheerful" translates the Greek ἱλαρός from which the English words "hilarity" and "hilarious" come. Christians are exhorted to be energetically cheerful givers. This exhortation is proper, for Christians should enjoy giving. Moreover, giving should bring great pleasure; it should be "an exhilarating experience." Hughes, 331.

[50] Hughes, 330. "Grudgingly" translates ἐκ λύπης (lit., "out of sorrow"). Paul Barrett translates "out of necessity" as "out of coercion." *The Second Epistle to the Corinthians* (Grand Rapids: Eerdmans, 1997), 437.

[51] Hughes, 330.

and prayerfully God's will concerning his giving. Furthermore, the Christian should not give a certain percentage just because someone has told him that he is duty bound to do so. God loves a cheerful giver. Therefore, He desires that Christians give willingly rather than dutifully. Giving "loses all its fragrance when the incense of a free and joyful spirit is wanting."[52] Therefore, the donor completely misses the joy and blessings of giving when he gives in a miserly way or because urged solely by public opinion or conscience.

Romans 12:8

Although all Christians form one body in Christ, not all Christians have the same spiritual gifts. For example, some have the gift of prophecy, others have the gift of teaching (vv. 6–7), and some have the gift of giving. To the Christian with the gift of giving, Paul says, "He that giveth, let him do it with simplicity." The believer with this gift "has the capacity to give of his substance to the work of the Lord or to the people of God, consistently, liberally, sacrificially, and with such wisdom and cheerfulness that others are encouraged and blessed."[53] Others are encouraged because he gives not only liberally, but with "purity of motive."[54]

---

[52] Hodge, *Second Epistle to the Corinthians*, 219.

[53] William McRae, *The Dynamics of Spiritual Gifts* (Grand Rapids: Zondervan, 1976), 50–51.

[54] Thus Charles Hodge translates ἁπλότητι. *Commentary on the Epistle to the Romans* (1886; repr., Grand Rapids: Eerdmans, 1974), 392. Often ἁπλότης denotes "purity of motive" or freedom from "pretense and dissimulation." Joseph Henry Thayer, trans., *A Greek-English Lexicon of the New Testament*, 4th ed. (1901; repr., Grand Rapids: Baker, 1977). See its use in 2 Cor. 1:12, Eph. 6:5, and Col. 3:22. However, it can also denote an "openness of heart manifesting itself by benefactions" (Thayer), and hence liberality (2 Cor. 8:2; 9:11, 13). Paul may well have intended a dual meaning for the word in Rom. 12:8. That is, the Christian with this spiritual gift should give generously and from pure motives.

Romans 12:13

Paul here enlarged the scope of his instructions about giving. In Romans 12:8 he treated the matter of giving by one who had a special spiritual gift. In this text he treated giving by all Christians, whether they have the spiritual gift or not. All believers, Paul suggested, should be "contributing to the needs of the saints, practicing hospitality" (NASB). Christians have a special obligation to one another. They are to share the financial burdens of one another. While giving to alleviate needs, those with financial means are to "fellowship" with those in need.[55] As usual, Paul emphasizes the proper manner and motive of giving rather than the amount.

Philippians 4:10–19

In these verses Paul expresses great appreciation for the generous beneficence of the Philippians. Paul apparently made no demands on them concerning giving. He delighted in their desire to help him financially (v. 10), but he preferred to learn contentment in both lean and prosperous times rather than to broadcast his financial state (vv. 11–13). Paul emphasized neither the proportion they gave nor the object of their giving (Paul was not seeking more money for himself) but the personal spiritual enrichment that their giving would produce (vv. 14–17).[56]

Titus 3:13–14

Paul concludes his instructions about giving with two related exhortations: "Diligently help Zenas the lawyer and Apollos on their way so that nothing is lacking for them. Our people must also learn to engage in good deeds to meet pressing needs, so that

---

[55] The word translated "contributing" (κοινωνέω) suggests much more than simply giving to meet a need. It connotes fellowship. Therefore it suggests that the Christian should so participate in his brother's needs that he feels a partnership and sympathy with him.

[56] Jac. J. Müller, *The Epistles of Paul to the Philippians and to Philemon* (Grand Rapids: Eerdmans, 1974), 150.

they will not be unfruitful" (NASB). Paul first exhorted Titus to personally and diligently outfit Zenas and Apollos for their journey.[57] Of course, Titus could not furnish everything, but he was to take responsibility for supplying the needs of the two Christian workers. But the responsibility to give did not stop with Titus, and others were to benefit from the giving besides Zenas and Apollos. All Christians ("our people") must "learn to engage in good deeds to meet pressing needs." The immediate need that Paul had in mind was to equip Zenas and Apollos, but the application is broader. The Christian must give, not only to supply the needs of God's ministers, but also to help any Christian with an urgent need.[58] Christians who thus act to help others in need will have fruitful lives.

CONCLUSION

A brief examination of Paul's teaching about Christian giving has shown that he does not emphasize or even directly mention tithing. Verses that bear most directly on Christian giving in general suggest giving in proportion to one's means.[59] Although the principle of proportionate giving is rooted in tithing, the proper carry-over of tithing to Christian times is not the strict giving of 10 percent, but the principle that one should regularly give a fixed proportion of one's income. Kellogg has astutely observed regarding 1 Corinthians 16:2 that

> [it] most clearly gives apostolic sanction to the fundamental principle of the tithe, namely that a definite portion of our income should be set apart for God. While, on the other hand, neither in this connection, where a mention of

---

[57] The word προπέμπω, translated "bring on their journey" (KJV) and "help on their way" (NASB), sometimes connotes the outfitting of a traveler "with the requisites for his journey" (Thayer).

[58] Donald Guthrie, *The Pastoral Epistles* (Grand Rapids: Eerdmans, 1976), 210.

[59] See the above discussion of 1 Cor. 16:2; 2 Cor. 8:12; and 9:6–7.

the law of the tithe might naturally have been expected, if it had been still binding as to the letter, nor in any other place does either the Apostle Paul or any other New Testament writer intimate that the Levitical law, requiring the precise proportion of a tenth, was still in force;—a fact which is the more noteworthy that so much is said on the duty of Christian benevolence.[60]

Therefore, whereas one Christian may conceivably meet his obligation to give by tithing, another wealthier Christian may need to give 25 percent or more in order to please God with his stewardship. Paul seems to summarize the proper method and manner of giving with the words, "Every man according as he purposeth in his heart, so let him give; not grudgingly, or of necessity: for God loveth a cheerful giver" (2 Cor. 9:7). This verse also emphasizes Paul's primary concern regarding Christian giving. He desired that Christians give from the proper motivation of joy. This does not mean that Christians should feel no obligation to give. They are obligated to support the work of God. Nevertheless, although Christians should recognize their duty to support the work of God, the overriding stimulus of all giving should be the joy of it, not the duty of it. As far as Paul is concerned, the Christian who dutifully tithes does not necessarily meet the biblical standards of stewardship. He may not have the proper motivation, and he may not be giving as God has prospered him. In the next chapter we will look more deeply into motivation as we focus on the joy of voluntary giving.

---

[60] S. H. Kellogg, *The Book of Leviticus*, 3rd ed. (1899; repr., Minneapolis: Klock and Klock, 1978), 563.

4

THE JOY OF VOLUNTARY GIVING

In the last chapter we surveyed much of the biblical data regarding a believer's giving to the Lord's work, especially as giving relates to the concept of tithing. We learned that the Bible gives both instructions and examples that allow for a broad understanding of a believer's giving responsibilities. Above all, a believer should view giving as a privilege, not a duty, and he should give as God has prospered him. In this chapter we want to dig deeper into the motivation of Christian giving by considering God's emphasis on giving voluntarily.

GOD OWNS ALL

Proponents of tithing usually make much of the idea that the tithe is a debt. According to this argument, tithing is not giving, but paying—paying a debt that one owes to God. "When we don't tithe," one man preaches, "we shirk a just debt."[1] Another preacher goes a step further. He believes that the tithe is not only a debt that the Christian ought to pay, but a debt that the Christian will pay, one way or the other. According to this man, God may go so far as to exact the debt in the form of a hospital bill.[2] But this is far-fetched and does not strengthen the argument for obligatory giving. Furthermore, obligatory giving is not the biblical emphasis.

---

[1] Billy Graham's sermon "Partners with God," cited by Jack Robinson, "Ten Percent," *Moody Monthly*, July–August 1970, 27.

[2] Malone, "Tithes of All," 2.

Often used to prove that the tithe is a debt is Moses' statement that "all the tithe of the land, whether of the seed of the land, or of the fruit of the tree, is the Lord's: it is holy unto the Lord" (Lev. 27:30). Indeed, this verse does indicate that the Israelite's tithe belonged to God. But Moses stated that the firstborn beast also belonged to the Lord (Lev. 27:26). Like the tithe, it could not be dedicated to the Lord by a vow, for it belonged to the Lord by law.[3] Therefore, if Christians are indebted to tithe, Christians are also indebted to give not only the firstborn of their flocks but also all of the other Levitical requirements. The application of the requirement of the firstborn to the average Christian today, who knows little of the nomadic life, is not only practically difficult but exegetically improper. Such an application would violate the New Testament teaching concerning the Christian's relation to the Law.[4] Nevertheless, the implication that one debt is just as binding as the other cannot be ignored. Either both debts are required of the Christian, or neither is. Only strained exegesis can make one obligation less incumbent upon the Christian than another. But rather than become entangled with an inconsistency or with an awkward application, most proponents of this argument for tithing ignore or miss the problem. And they fail to relate adequately the universal ownership of God to this fact that the tithe belongs to God.[5] That is, although God does have a legitimate claim to the tithe, He also has a legitimate claim to all that a Christian has.[6] In a sense the Christian can give God nothing, for God owns everything to begin with. Therefore, the Christian is indebted in

---

[3] *KD, Pentateuch*, 2:484.

[4] For an excellent, balanced treatment of the Christian's relationship to the Law, see Ken Casillas, *The Law and the Christian* (Greenville, SC: Bob Jones University Press, 2007).

[5] See Ps. 24:1; 50:12; 89:11; and 1 Cor. 10:26 for proof of God's absolute ownership of the world.

[6] Jesus acquainted the rich young ruler with this claim (Mark 10:17–23).

principle to give all to God. As Jesus said, "Whosoever he be of you that forsaketh not *all* that he hath, he cannot be my disciple" (Luke 14:33).

BIBLICAL EMPHASIS ON VOLUNTARY GIVING

Throughout Scripture, God encourages voluntary giving much more often than He does obligatory giving. No record of required giving exists before the time of Moses, and yet God's people gave. Evidently they gave because they wanted to and not because they were required to. Examples of such joyful giving occur throughout Old and New Testament history.

Old Testament Voluntary Giving

Job, for example, compassionately and willingly gave of his substance to the poor and needy (Job 31:16–23). Likewise Abraham tithed the spoils of his victory because he wanted to honor and please God (Gen. 14:17–20; Heb. 7:1–10). One of the most instructive accounts of voluntary giving particularly emphasizes God's pleasure with such giving. Having just come down from Mount Sinai, Moses received this instruction from God: "Tell the sons of Israel to raise a contribution for Me; from every man whose heart moves him you shall raise My contribution" (Exod. 25:2, NASB). Significantly, in this first biblical record of explicit direction for giving, God shows His preference for voluntary contributions over required contributions. Since Israel needed the tabernacle for the establishment of the proper worship of Jehovah, the Lord could have required each person to contribute something for its construction. But instead the Lord allowed for and even encouraged voluntary contributions. Those, and by implication only those, whose hearts moved them were to bring contributions. The emphasis upon freewill contributions apparently pleased the people, for they brought much more than enough (Exod. 36:5–7). Consequently, a great lesson lies here for those who, possibly fearing a lack of funds, promote obligatory giving. When God's people clearly understand a need and are living in fellowship with Him, they will give cheerfully and generously. Encouraging God's people to give proportionately and voluntarily is the best way to obtain abundant provisions for the work of the Lord.

The principle of voluntary giving appears even in a context about tithing. The Mosaic Law required no one to do so, but by special vow many Israelites voluntarily dedicated to God their children, their beasts, their dwellings, and their land (Lev. 27:1–29). These verses explain what an Israelite could properly dedicate to God, and under what conditions he could obtain release from the vow of dedication. However, the key idea for the present discussion is simply that these dedications were spontaneous manifestations of reverence and love for God. Of course, God took the dedicatory vows by the Israelites seriously. He expected them to be fulfilled. But He did not command that the Israelites vow to dedicate something to Him. Theirs was the privilege, not the duty, to do so.

Another example of voluntary giving, similar to that of contributions for the tabernacle, is set near the end of David's life (1 Chron. 29:1–9). David himself had exemplified to the people a great generosity. Because of his delight in the prospect of the temple, David provided for its construction out of his own private fortune (vv. 3–5), besides what he provided in his official capacity as king (v. 2). But by himself David could not completely furnish the temple, so he called upon the people to make voluntary contributions. No doubt David remembered the method of Moses and its good results when Moses raised contributions for the tabernacle (Exod. 25:2; 36:3–7). Therefore David encouraged the people to follow his own model of voluntary liberality with the question: "Who then is willing to consecrate himself this day to the Lord?" (v. 5*b*, NASB). Two facts suggest that this was an encouragement to give.

First, the phrase "to consecrate himself" literally reads "to fill his hand" and connotes the bringing of an offering to God.[7] Also, the response of the people to give willingly demonstrates how they interpreted David's question (vv. 6–8). So again the Scriptures emphasize voluntary giving. The beauty of voluntary giving is that it elicits the highest and the most purely motivated responses. Those who contribute voluntarily do so not grudgingly, but because their hearts delight in such giving. As the Chronicler puts it, they give "with perfect heart" (v. 9).

Centuries after David began to build the temple, a remnant of devout Jews returned with Ezra to their ravaged homeland. Seeing the house of the Lord destroyed, these enthusiasts determined of their own accord to restore it (Ezra 2:68–69). Two aspects of their giving stand out: they gave "freely" (2:68), and they gave "after their ability" (2:69). Both aspects suggest voluntary giving: the donor gave uncompelled, and he gave according to his means, as he determined those means.[8] Similarly, a few years later, Nehemiah, other leaders, and the people willingly gave to the Lord's work (Neh. 7:70–72). In both instances people gave because the realization of the great need moved their hearts to respond.

New Testament Voluntary Giving

Whereas the Old Testament often mentions voluntary giving, the New Testament emphasizes voluntary giving almost exclusively. Even New Testament passages that mention tithing do not emphasize it. The Lord spotlighted the Pharisees' neglect of the moral standards of Judaism, not their scrupulous tithing (Matt. 23:23; Luke 11:42). Furthermore, the only other reference to Pharisaic tithing is hardly a commendation of the practice (Luke 18:12). The

---

[7] KD, Chronicles, 297.

[8] The word translated "freely" (נדב) "connotes an uncompelled and free movement of the will unto divine service or sacrifice." TWOT, 2:554.

tithing Pharisee left the temple unjustified before God because he proudly thought scrupulosity over matters like tithing made him acceptable to God (18:11, 14). Finally, the passage in Hebrews highlights the greatness of the priestly order of Melchizedek, not the tithing of Abraham (Heb. 6:20–7:10). In contrast to the scanty reference to compulsory giving, the New Testament repeatedly endorses voluntary giving both by commending those who do it and by direct statement.

The Israelites, and possibly all of those whom the New Testament commends for giving, contributed more than a tithe. Moreover, nowhere do the Scriptures state that a generous contributor consciously tithed and then gave more as an offering.

Zacchaeus furnished the first New Testament example of commendable voluntary giving. His initial response to the Lord after his salvation was, "Behold, Lord, the half of my goods I give to the poor; and if I have taken any thing from any man by false accusation, I restore him fourfold" (Luke 19:8). Zacchaeus proposed to give far more than 10 percent; in fact he promised to give 50 percent of his possessions to the poor. This percentage did not include what he might give for the support of ministers and a place of worship. Obviously, Jesus commends this manner of giving, for He took the response of Zacchaeus as an indication of genuine salvation (19:9).

Another exemplar of voluntary giving is the humble widow (Luke 21:1–4; Mark 12:41–44). Although she gave only "two mites," Jesus has stamped her offering with divine approval (Luke 21:3–4). This impoverished widow surpassed Zacchaeus, for she gave 100 percent of what she had to live on at the time. That she gave all she had might seem foolish, but her gift pleased God, Who looks more at the spirit motivating the gift than at its amount. Clearly, God is interested not nearly so much in giving out of a sense of duty as He is in spontaneous, heartfelt giving. That Jesus viewed her gift as more valuable than that of all the others taken together (v. 3*b*) strongly suggests God's attitude toward motivation in giving.

Like Zacchaeus and the widow, Mary expressed her love to the Lord in an unusual way (Matt. 26:6–13). Having saved some expensive perfume in a costly alabaster flask, she anointed Jesus and thus performed one of the noblest acts of giving of all time. In contrast to the irate disciples who criticized her for apparent wastefulness (vv. 8–9), Jesus promised to immortalize her act (v. 13). Latent in Jesus' commendation is His recognition of an important principle concerning heartfelt giving. The principle is that any act of earnest giving is useful; although it may seem impractical, it naturally inspires others to similar action. Broadus elaborates: "This unpractical gift, and the Saviour's commendation of it, have themselves caused richer gifts to the poor in all ages than the wealth of Jerusalem would have equaled."[9]

Luke's accounts of the giving by the believers in Jerusalem further prove that spontaneous giving inspires others to give. But more importantly, they add more evidence that the New Testament emphasizes voluntary giving. The first account reads, "And all that believed were together, and had all things common; and sold their possessions and goods, and parted them to all men, as every man had need" (Acts 2:44–45). These Christians exhibited a magnanimous, fraternal spirit. They desired to help one another in a very practical way. Having sold their real estate and their goods and then having pooled their resources, they distributed them to meet the continually arising needs of the assembly. Whether or not each

[9] Broadus, *Matthew*, 521.

believer sold all of his possessions is unclear.[10] But that each gave cheerfully and voluntarily is plain. These believers continued their practice for a time, for in Luke's second account he writes, "Neither was there any among them that lacked: for as many as were possessors of lands or houses sold them, and brought the prices of the things that were sold, and laid them down at the apostles' feet" (4:34–35a). These Christians could hardly keep from giving. The apostles applied no coercion; the motivating force was the anointed apostolic preaching along with the abundant grace upon them all (4:33).

Outstanding examples of sacrificial giving, such as that of Barnabas, further inspired the people to give generously and freely (4:36–37).[11] If for no other reason, we know that these believers were not practicing communism (in today's sense of a totalitarian society) because they willingly sold their property and donated the proceeds. As Peter told Ananias concerning the right of private ownership and distribution, "While it remained unsold, did it not remain your own? And after it was sold, was it not under your control?" (5:4a, NASB). Many of these believers were Jews, who certainly would have known the teaching of the Old Testament about tithing.[12] Nevertheless, their giving was not that of tithing but of giving in some cases all that they owned (4:32).

Luke also commends two others for their voluntary giving: Dorcas (Acts 9:36–39) and Cornelius (Acts 10:2–4). Dorcas was "full of good works and almsdeeds" (9:36). As one who gave willingly and

---

[10] Craig Blomberg references others who support the idea that "there is no once-for-all divestiture of property in view here, but periodic acts of charity as needs arose." *Neither Poverty Nor Riches* (Downers Grove: Intervarsity Press, 1999), 162.

[11] In this way Barnabas lived up to his appellation, which means "son of encouragement."

[12] Most of Peter's 3000 converts were Jews or proselytes to Judaism who had come to Jerusalem to keep the feast of Pentecost (2:5–10, 41).

sacrificially, she gave not only money but also time and effort. She evidently bought material with her own money, made "coats and garments," and then gave them away to needy widows and others (9:39). To her, giving was a privilege, an opportunity for doing a good work and showing mercy.[13] Thus her testimony of loving and sacrificial giving endeared her to many (9:39). Cornelius, whom Luke also recognized as a generous giver, was an Italian and an adherent to Judaism (Acts 10:2–4).[14] He may have tithed according to Jewish law, but the passage does not mention that he did. However, the passage reveals that he practiced one of Judaism's great virtues, the giving of alms (vv. 2, 4). His many charitable deeds of mercy especially benefited "the Jewish people" (10:2, NASB). The passage gives no details about the kinds of alms Cornelius practiced, but apparently his charity met many kinds of needs. One fact is certain: God delighted in the benevolence of Cornelius, for God took note of it as He would the smoke of a burnt offering.[15]

Paul continued the New Testament's emphasis on voluntary giving. A survey of his teaching has already been made and need not be repeated. The conclusion offered previously from Paul's statement (2 Cor. 9:7) is applicable here: Christians should give cheerfully and voluntarily, not grudgingly or dutifully. Besides, the first responsibility of the Christian is to dedicate himself to God (2 Cor. 8:5), not to give simply out of a sense of duty.

With the practice of Gaius, the Apostle John concludes the record of those who are commended for giving. John praised Gaius

---

[13] The last clause of 9:36 literally reads, "and merciful deeds [ἐλεημοσυνῶν—derived from the word for mercy, ἔλεος] which she was doing." Her merciful deeds were the giving of clothes to needy people.

[14] He was a God-fearer (10:2). God-fearers were not proselytes in the strict sense of the term. They appreciated the monotheism and ethical standards of Judaism but had not submitted to circumcision. For a fuller discussion see F. F. Bruce, *Commentary on the Book of the Acts* (Grand Rapids: Eerdmans, 1973), 64, 216.

[15] Ibid.

for faithfully providing the needs of itinerant missionaries who received no support from the unsaved (3 John 5–8). Although John determined that Christians are obligated to exhibit fraternal hospitality (v. 8), he based the obligation on the nature of Christian brotherhood and the need to spread the truth, rather than on the idea that Christians owe a tithe to God.

To review, Zacchaeus (Luke 19:8), the poor widow (Luke 21:1–4), and the Christians in Jerusalem (Acts 2:44–45; 4:32–37) gave much more than a tithe. Furthermore, Mary (Matt. 26:6–13), Dorcas (Acts 9:36–39), Cornelius (Acts 10:1–4), the Macedonian Christians (2 Cor. 8–9), and Gaius (3 John 5–8) may all have given more than a tithe. Since these are the ones who received commendation for their giving, one may legitimately infer that God would have Christians emulate their practice. Not giving as a duty, but giving out of love for God and concern for the needs of others, is the emphasis of the New Testament. As Jesus revealed in His analysis of the widow's giving (Luke 21:1–4), the question is not the exact percentage that one gives but the sacrificial quality of one's giving.[16]

God's Promises to Bless

The key text here and the one that proponents of tithing have perhaps used most often to challenge believers regarding tithing is Malachi 3:10:

> Bring ye all the tithes into the storehouse, that there may be meat in mine house, and prove me now herewith, saith the Lord of hosts, if I will not open you the windows of heaven, and pour you out a blessing, that there shall not be room enough to receive it."

---

[16] 2 Cor. 8:2–3 also demonstrates God's high valuation of sacrificial giving. The Macedonian Christians gave generously out of their deep poverty.

Malachi accused the people of robbing God by not giving the tithes (and offerings) as they should (vv. 8–10). Then he offered God's promise of blessing if they would renew their tithe payments in full. However, to conclude that Christians should tithe because of the blessing of tithing mentioned here is improper for two reasons. First, the refutation of the argument that Christians should tithe because Moses commanded tithing also applies here. Malachi evidently meant for each one to bring all three of the tithes required of him, and not just 10 percent of his income.[17] In other words, in order to be accurate, one must argue that Christians should give at least 20 percent in order to be blessed. Furthermore, those who argue on the basis of this verse that Christians should tithe overlook the fact that the Jews were robbing God of offerings as well as tithes (v. 8). Therefore, the argument should be that God blesses those (and those only) who give both tithes and offerings.

The proponents of this argument have little else to propose besides the reference in Malachi. They sometimes argue that God has blessed tithers, and they give testimonies to prove it. However, one could just as forcefully argue that God has blessed those who give more than 10 percent. Indeed, many have testified of God's ever-increasing blessings as they have increased the percentage of their giving.[18] Similarly, the New Testament references to God's promises concerning giving suggest that God blesses in proportion to one's liberality. For example, Luke records this astounding promise:

> Give, and it shall be given unto you; good measure, pressed down, and shaken together, and running over, shall men

---

[17] See "Moses' Commands" above for a discussion of the three tithes that Moses commanded. Charles Feinberg convincingly argues that the Israelites were delinquent in giving the three tithes and other offerings. *The Minor Prophets* (Chicago: Moody Press, 1976), 263.

[18] See, for example, A. T. Pierson's *George Müller of Bristol*, 444–45.

give into your bosom. For with the same measure that ye mete withal it shall be measured to you again (6:38).

Paul restates the same promise: "He which soweth sparingly shall reap also sparingly; and he which soweth bountifully shall reap also bountifully" (2 Cor. 9:6). The point of these verses seems to have nothing to do with tithing but with the blessed consequence of generous giving.[19]

CONCLUSION

The biblical basis for enjoining tithing on Christians is meager. Abraham and Jacob tithed before Moses mandated tithing. Thus the principle of giving one tenth to God is partially applicable today, in that Christians can use a tenth as a starting point, and they should give proportionally. *The Scriptures never indicate that the principle of tithing has been abolished.* However, the Mosaic regulations concerning tithing have been abolished, since Christianity has superseded the Mosaic system of worship. Moreover, that Christians live under grace rather than under Mosaic Law suggests that they should give even more than the Jews did. A higher motivation—the glory of God through His grace exhibited in the work of Christ—should elicit a higher response.

Paul laid a basis for the conclusion that Christians should give more than the Jews did. He stated that "the law was our schoolmaster to bring us unto Christ" (Gal. 3:24a). That is, the Mosaic Law served as a guardian and disciplinarian to regulate the conduct of God's people until the time when strict supervision was no longer needed.[20] Therefore, Christians are free from the Mosaic

---

[19] This principle should not be confused with the "prosperity gospel." God does not necessarily return physical and financial benefits on all who give to Him; and more importantly, God's people give not in order to get more, but in order to show their love for God and their gratitude for His grace to them.

[20] William Hendriksen, *New Testament Commentary: Exposition of Galatians* (Grand Rapids: Baker, 1968), 148; J. B. Lightfoot, *The Epistle of St. Paul to the Galatians*

Law, but bound by the higher, "royal law" (James 2:8) of love to Christ and others. Because this higher law is based on love rather than on duty, the Christian has a higher motivation than did the Jew. Consequently God expects more of the Christian than He did of the Jew. Greater privilege and freedom is not a license for indolence but a stimulus for greater consecration and sacrifice. Having properly understood that he has benefited immeasurably and eternally from God's marvelous, saving grace, a Christian will concern himself not with giving a minimum but with giving a maximum.

Although tithing may be a legitimate Christian practice, it is not the biblical emphasis. One looks in vain for an emphasis on tithing in the New Testament. The teaching of the New Testament, and particularly the epistles, which, according to proven rules of biblical interpretation, provide the norms for Christian practice, may be summarized as follows: (1) Christians should give sacrificially (Luke 21:1–4; Acts 2:44–45; 4:34–37; 2 Cor. 8:2–3); (2) Christians should give systematically (1 Cor. 16:2); (3) Christians should give proportionally (1 Cor. 16:2; cf. 2 Cor. 8:12); (4) Christians should give generously (2 Cor. 9:6, 13); (5) Christians should give voluntarily and cheerfully (2 Cor. 9:7); and (6) Christians should give believingly, trusting God to supply all needs (Phil. 4:19; 2 Cor. 9:8; cf. Luke 6:38). Noticeably absent from the data is a regimented system of giving.

Certainly the Christian is *responsible* to give, but the better statement of Christian giving is that the Christian has the *joy* and *privilege* of giving. As he gives within the broad guidelines listed above, the believer will experience deep satisfaction and bring upon himself God's fullest blessings. His motivation for giving should not be a sense of duty but a sense of gratitude. A Christian who grasps

(Grand Rapids: Zondervan, 1978), 148–49.

that God, Who spared not His own Son but gave Him up as a ransom for sinners, will "freely give us all things" (Rom. 8:32), will also freely and cheerfully give of his possessions. Such voluntary and joyful giving will amply provide for Christian causes as well as bring delight to God, Who "loves a cheerful giver."

5

A BIBLICAL VIEW OF DEBT

Two trillion, four hundred and forty billion dollars. Can you comprehend this amount of money? It is the total U. S. consumer debt as of April 2010.[1] In other words, if you are an average American, your personal debt load is approaching eight thousand dollars. But that is not all. In addition to consumer debt, Americans are also loaded down with a national debt of over $14 trillion,[2] or around forty-six thousand dollars per person. If you want a sobering and scary reality check regarding national debt, go to the website www.usdebtclock.org and see the numbers rapidly and constantly changing to reflect our ever-growing servitude to our creditors. If there has ever been a time in America's history when we needed to heed biblical instruction regarding indebtedness, this is that time. But it is not just America and Americans who have a debt problem. The large front-page headline of the *Wall Street Journal* on April 7, 2011, screamed "Portugal Pleads for Rescue."[3] Portugal had become the third nation in the euro zone to beg for help in containing its sovereign-debt crisis. So for numerous reasons such as easy credit, impulse buying, greedy presumption about real estate values, and the enticement of the worldly philosophy of enjoying now and paying later, Americans and many others

---

[1] Source: Federal Reserve's G.19 report of consumer credit, June 2010. http://www.creditcards.com/credit-card-news/credit-card-industry-facts-personal-debt-statistics-1276.php.

[2] http://www.usdebtclock.org.

[3] *The Wall Street Journal*, 7 April 2011, sec. A, p. 1.

are drowning in debt with the shore of deliverance almost out of sight. We desperately need a biblical understanding of indebtedness as we seek to make informed financial decisions in a world awash in red ink.

DEFINITION OF DEBT

First, let's define what we are talking about. Strictly speaking, one is in debt when one purchases something without paying for it immediately. However, nearly everyone contracts with the telephone or power company to receive services that are not paid for immediately. The well-known Christian money management advisor Larry Burkett offers this useful definition of debt: "The scriptural definition of debt is the inability to meet agreed-upon obligations. When a person buys something on credit, that is not necessarily a debt; it is a contract. But, when the terms of that contract are violated, scriptural debt occurs."[4]

Therefore, purchasing on credit or becoming liable for something such as a power bill is not inherently wrong. It may be legitimate *if* one has the available means to honor the terms. In an earlier book Burkett proposed that excessive debt occurs when one makes an agreement with terms one is not able to meet or when one has payments past due for goods or services or when one's financial obligations cause anxiety or unmet family needs.[5] The following treatment will prove him generally correct. However, since the Bible and common sense offer caution against indebtedness, the better definition of excessive debt is that which occurs when any one of the biblical or practical cautions go unheeded.[6] If a

---

[4] Larry Burkett, *The Complete Guide to Managing Your Money* (New York: Inspirational Press, 1996), 41.

[5] *Your Finances in Changing Times* (n.p.: Christian Financial Concepts, 1975), 83.

[6] Financial advisor Ron Blue suggests a similar approach. He gives four strict criteria to determine whether a debt is acceptable: (1) Does it make economic sense to incur the debt? (2) Are *both* spouses free from any anxiety regarding this debt? (3) Can the

Christian cannot or will not heed the cautions before going into debt, the result will be unnecessary or excessive debt. Ultimately, excessive debt comes down to the heart issue of contentment. If we are obeying the admonition to be "content with such things as [we] have" (Heb. 13:5), we will not buy what we cannot afford. Admittedly, biblical encouragements to lend suggest that debt is not strictly taboo. Nevertheless, in every case the Lord commends lending money, not borrowing it.

As suggested above, the concept of indebtedness in Scripture has both positive and negative aspects. From the creditor's side, there are encouragements to lend. From the debtor's side, there are numerous cautions. When the financially capable do not lend, they sometimes miss opportunities for ministering to needy brethren. Because of this opportunity for the Christian, the Scriptures encourage the judicious lending of money or other items to those in genuine need.

DEBT PROPRIETY

Because the Lord encourages judicious lending, a logical inference is that a needy brother may legitimately incur some indebtedness. Giving one example of debt propriety, the Psalmist encouraged judicious lending when he wrote, "A good man sheweth favour, and lendeth: he will guide his affairs with discretion" (Ps. 112:5). Blessedness comes to the unselfish man.[7] The happy man is "gracious" (NASB), and he manifests his graciousness by a willingness

---

debt be undertaken with spiritual peace of mind? (4) I ask myself "What 'God-given' goals and objectives am I meeting with this debt that can be met in no other way?" See *The New Master Your Money* (Chicago: Moody, 2004), 72–73.

[7] H. C. Leupold, *Exposition of the Psalms* (Grand Rapids: Baker, 1969), 787.

to lend[8] to those in need. Lending, then, is a merciful deed.[9] This passage portrays lending not as a "commercial operation" but as a pure "act of charity."[10] Although the last clause intimates that the lender should be discreet in his lending,[11] it does not lessen the gracious quality of the lending act. This commendation of lending implies that some people legitimately need to borrow money, presumably to meet basic needs.

What the Psalmist commends, Moses both commends and commands. Moses enjoins the merciful act of lending when it helps those in need. For example, Moses told his people: "Now in case a countryman of yours becomes poor and his means with regard to you falter, then you are to sustain him, like a stranger or a sojourner, that he may live with you" (Lev. 25:35, NASB). Although this verse does not mention lending, the next verse establishes the lending context, for the lender was not to "take usurious interest" (NASB) from the borrower.[12] The prosperous Israelite might tend to put off helping his brother because the Jubilee was not far off.[13] Therefore, Moses exhorted him not to think selfishly, but to help the poor brother by lending him money or food (v. 37). If

---

[8] Leupold (786) translates לוה "ready to lend." Also, according to *TWOT*, 1:471, "willingness to lend was a sign of righteous graciousness."

[9] The Psalmist further explains that the righteous man is "ever merciful, and lendeth" (37:26a).

[10] Joseph Addison Alexander, *The Psalms Translated and Explained* (1873; repr., Grand Rapids: Baker, 1977), 464.

[11] Charles H. Spurgeon says that a good man will lend "judiciously where a loan will be of permanent service." *The Treasury of David* (Grand Rapids: Zondervan, 1976), 3:17.

[12] Other references to laws against interest from fellow Israelites are Exod. 22:25–27 and Deut. 23:19–20.

[13] Lev. 25 deals with both the sabbatical year, the year of rest for the land following six productive years, and the year of Jubilee, the year of great release enjoyed every fifty years. The law concerning the year of Jubilee had numerous provisions but one major aim: to reunite property owners with their land. J[ohn] Lilley, "Jubilee Year," *ZPEB* (1976), 3:715. See also Andrew A. Bonar, *A Commentary on the Book of Leviticus* (1851; repr., Grand Rapids: Zondervan, 1959), 462.

the brother became unable to sustain himself without help, the favored Israelite was not to demand interest on a monetary loan or additional food on a provisional loan.[14] Instead he was to glory in the opportunity to help a needy brother. He was to let his redemption produce openheartedness toward others.[15]

Moses reiterates the necessity and blessing of lending to poorer brethren in Deuteronomy 15:7–8:

> If there is a poor man with you, one of your brothers, in any of your towns in your land which the Lord your God is giving you, you shall not harden your heart, nor close your hand from your poor brother; but you shall freely open your hand to him, and shall generously lend him sufficient for his need in whatever he lacks (NASB).

With this dictate God encourages unselfish and compassionate benevolence. The Israelite was to give even though the sabbatical year was near (v. 9).[16] To begrudge helping the poor brother, and thus to give him nothing, was sin (v. 9).[17] A loan helped a needy brother, but it also helped the gracious lender. God promised to

---

[14] Bonar, 462.

[15] The national redemption, God's bringing them "out of the land of Egypt" (Lev. 25:38), symbolized individual redemption. Bonar (462) notes the relationship between redemption and openheartedness toward others.

[16] The sabbatical year brought either a complete remission of the debt or a one-year suspension of the right to demand payment. Scholars have not decided conclusively on either choice, but it makes little difference. Either way the creditor naturally resisted lending but was not to let selfish considerations govern his actions.

[17] Although poor Israelites had a divinely instituted right to loans from wealthier brethren, this right had its limits. In Exod. 22:25–27, Moses states that the wealthy Israelite could require collateral from the borrower, but the creditor had to return the collateral by nightfall. The collateral benefited the creditor only indirectly. Its main function was to limit the indebtedness that a borrower could assume. The borrower could not simultaneously use his possession as collateral for two loans. Therefore, the biblical regulations limited the amount of legitimate indebtedness to one's immediate assets. Gary North, *An Introduction to Christian Economics* ([Nutley, NJ]: The Craig Press, 1976), 9–10.

bless the lender in all his "work" and in all his "undertakings" (v. 10, NASB). Note, however, that this command applies to benevolence lending and not to commercial lending, for no interest was allowed (Lev. 25:36–37), and the entire debt was cancelled every seventh (sabbatical) year.

Christ too commands lending: "Give to him that asketh thee, and from him that would borrow of thee turn not thou away" (Matt. 5:42). He directs that Christians be willing both to give and to lend, even when it might be unpleasant to do so.[18] However, Jesus did not intend this as an absolute injunction. God Himself gives only when He deems it proper. "To give," Broadus says, "to those who 'ask amiss' (James 4:3) would be no real kindness to them— nor to us."[19] Barnes too offers some sensible advice for applying this text:

> The rule must be interpreted so as to be consistent with our duty to our families, (1 Tim. 5:8) and with other objects of justice and charity. It is seldom, perhaps never, good to give to a man that is able to work (2 Th. 3:10). To give to such is to encourage laziness, and to support the idle at the expense of the industrious. If such a man is indeed hungry, feed him; if he wants anything farther, give him employment. If a widow, an orphan, a man of misfortune, or a man infirm, lame, or sick, is at your door, never send them away empty.[20]

Although the passage emphasizes ready assistance in answer to distress calls, Christ does not mean for Christians to promote

---

[18] Broadus, *Matthew*, 120.

[19] Ibid., 121.

[20] Albert Barnes, *Notes on the New Testament: Matthew and Mark*, ed. Robert Frew (Grand Rapids: Baker, 1979), 60.

"shiftlessness, dishonesty and greed."[21] Still, Christ encourages lending because it can help those in need.

Christ restates the imperative to lend in Luke 6:34–35:

> And if ye lend to them of whom ye hope to receive, what thank have ye? For sinners also lend to sinners, to receive as much again. But love ye your enemies, and do good, and lend, hoping for nothing again; and your reward shall be great, and ye shall be the children of the Highest: for he is kind unto the unthankful and to the evil.

In this discussion of the test for genuine love, Jesus shows that there is nothing particularly gracious about showing kindness to kind benefactors. Even "sinners" do that. A Christian manifests real love by unselfish kindness to those who are ungrateful and hateful. One avenue of unselfish kindness is to lend without despairing over the likelihood of getting nothing back.[22] This means that sometimes the believer should be prepared to view the loan in essence as a gift. The believer is to offer compassionate, discerning help to the hopeless.[23] Jesus also recognized the benefits accruing to the lender when He stated, "your reward shall be great" (6:35). In other words, the Lord gives spiritual blessings, and sometimes

---

[21] Lenski, *St. Matthew's Gospel*, 244.

[22] The KJV translation of μηδὲν ἀπελπίζοντες ("hoping for nothing again") is interpretive. R. C. H. Lenski maintains that ἀπελπίζω nowhere else means "hoping for nothing in the way of return." Nevertheless he admits this as the meaning here because of the logic required. Jesus contrasts the disciples' lending with that of the sinners. Sinners lend only to those who will pay them back; Christ's disciples should sometimes lend without looking for repayment. *St. Luke's Gospel*, 370.

[23] "By 'never despairing' or 'giving up nothing in despair' Jesus means that we are not to despair about getting the money back. We are to help the apparently hopeless cases. Medical writers use the word for desperate or hopeless cases." A. T. Robertson, *Word Pictures in the New Testament: The Gospel According to Luke*, vol. 3 (Nashville: Broadman, 1930), 92.

material blessings, to those who love the needy. Furthermore, generous lending to the ungodly proves that one is a true son of God.[24]

In His parable of the friends at midnight (Luke 11:5–8), Jesus indirectly approves lending. Having learned of an unexpected guest, the host went to his friend and said: "Friend, lend me three loaves" (11:5).[25] That the importunate friend really needed the bread suggests again that borrowing is not strictly prohibited. Sometimes men do have legitimate needs that only a temporary loan can meet, and that lending may well amount to giving away, for in a situation like this the lender would not likely expect a repayment.

To sum up, the Scriptures occasionally encourage or even require lending to those in need. A valid inference, then, is that one may sometimes need to borrow money or goods for pressing needs. However, the Scriptures we surveyed mention borrowing only for needs (not luxuries), and pressing needs at that. Also, the Bible commends lending because it can be a righteous deed and because it can help those in need. The tenor of all applicable passages is

---

[24] Two observations prove that Jesus envisioned lending to sinners, rather than to saints: (1) the verse calls for the Christian to love his "enemies," who logically must be non-Christians, and (2) Jesus exhorts Christians to emulate God the Father, Who is kind to "ungrateful and evil men" (NASB); William Hendriksen, *New Testament Commentary: Exposition of the Gospel According to Luke* (Grand Rapids: Baker, 1978), 354.

[25] The word for lend, χράω, occurs only here in the New Testament. The verb "to lend" in Matt. 5:42 and Luke 6:34 (2) and 6:35 is δανίζω. Joseph Henry Thayer makes a distinction between χράω (κίχρημι) and δανίζω (sometimes spelled δανείζω). The former means "to grant the use of, as a friendly act." The latter means "to lend on interest as a business transaction." *Greek-English Lexicon*, 125. M. R. Vincent agrees that δανείζω denotes to lend with interest. *Word Studies in the New Testament* (McLean, VA: MacDonald Publishing Company, n.d.), 1:163. That Christ encouraged lending at interest is noteworthy. Nearly all of the major early church fathers—Tertullian, Basil, Ambrose, Chrysostom and Jerome, to name a few—condemned usury, that is, charging interest or making a profit on a loan. Robert Maloney, "The Teaching of the Fathers on Usury: An Historical Study on the Development of Christian Thinking," *Vigiliae Christianae*, XXVII (1973), 241–65. The Fathers considered usury to be forbidden in the Old Testament (cf. Ps. 15:5), and "incompatible with Christian love" (Maloney, 242). However, it seems they never wrestled with the possibility that δανείζω could mean to lend with interest and that Christ recommended such lending in Matt. 5:42.

that of compassion. The Christian lender should loan primarily in order to help someone in financial straits rather than to make a profit from interest charges. Passages that seem to deal with commercial lending are excluded here, for they do not necessarily suggest debt propriety but rather show that the Israelites had the right to expect interest from foreigners in business transactions (e.g., Deut. 23:20). The Psalmist's words are appropriate again because they summarize the key thought of this section: "A good man sheweth favor, and lendeth" (112:5*a*).

BIBLICAL CAUTIONS[26]

Although the Bible condones borrowing, it never recommends it.[27] The Scriptures consistently portray debt as something unfortunate and to avoid whenever possible. Besides biblical cautions against indebtedness, one must also heed practical cautions against it. As already shown, personal and national indebtedness has reached such staggering proportions that no one, but especially not believers, can afford to ignore or minimize these cautions. A person or nation who refuses to consider seriously any one of the following biblical or practical cautions will end up with excessive indebtedness at best and possibly even utter financial disaster.

Debt Servitude

> For the Lord thy God blesseth thee, as he promised thee: and thou shalt lend unto many nations, but thou shalt not borrow; and thou shalt reign over many nations, but they shall not reign over thee (Deut. 15:6).

---

[26] The reader should note that not all of the biblical cautions are directly applicable today. For example, imprisonment for debtors (Luke 12:58–59) is highly unlikely with today's bankruptcy laws. However, the biblical cautions are important because they demonstrate what can happen in a society and because they illustrate how God views most indebtedness. Besides, a return to stricter laws against debtors is always possible.

[27] In the following discussion, borrowing, debt, and indebtedness are synonymous.

Here Moses describes the Lord's promised blessing upon Israel in its financial aspect. The Lord would evince His favor by placing the "many nations" in financial servitude to Israel. Israel would know they were her servants, because they would have to borrow from her. Because of her "financial and material superiority," Israel would rule over the nations.[28] Not Israel, but the nations, would endure the servant's role.[29] With similar wording Moses repeats this idea that an obedient Israel would enjoy financial superiority over the nations (Deut. 28:12). However, a disobedient Israel would find a reversal of roles. Describing the nations' role as ruler and Israel's role as servant, Moses prophesied, "He [the stranger, the resident-alien Canaanite whom Israel had dispossessed; contrast verses 12–13] shall lend to thee, and thou shalt not lend to him: he shall be the head, and thou shalt be the tail" (28:44).[30] The metaphorical appendage, "he shall be the head, and thou shalt be the tail," plainly depicts the creditor as the borrower's master. Being the "head" and not the "tail," "above" and not "beneath," the creditor dictates to the borrower.

What Moses states indirectly, the writer of Proverbs states explicitly: "The rich rules over the poor, and the borrower becomes the lender's slave" (22:7, NASB).[31] Proverbs confirms what many have learned from experience: "Contracting a debt brings naturally with it a slavish relation of dependence."[32] "A man has," says

---

[28] Driver, *Deuteronomy*, 176.

[29] Craigie, *The Book of Deuteronomy*, 237.

[30] Note that Moses had stated the reverse in 28:12; see J. A. Thompson, *Deuteronomy* (London: Inter-Varsity Press, 1974), 275, for a discussion of the antecedent of "he" in the verse.

[31] "Slave" is a better translation of עֶבֶד than "servant" (KJV). *TWOT*, 2:639, says that "the most basic idea of עֶבֶד is that of slave."

[32] *KD, Proverbs*, 2:87.

George Lawson, "as many masters as he has creditors."[33] The position of debt servitude is dangerous for the Christian. God warns the Christian not to be any man's servant (1 Cor. 7:23), but to maintain freedom to serve Christ.

Jesus, too, portrays indebtedness as a type of slavery. He explains the creditor's response to the pleading debtor: "Then the lord of that servant was moved with compassion, and loosed him, and forgave him the debt" (Matt. 18:27). This verse compares release from slavery ("he loosed him") with release from debt. Release from slavery and getting out of debt are not necessarily synonymous.[34] However, the word choice is instructive. The verb "to release" often connotes a release from bondage.[35] Thus Christ recognized that the debtor invariably takes the role of a servant.

When we take into account the biblical warnings as well as the practical outworking of dealing with indebtedness, we can only acknowledge that indeed "the borrower *is* [emphasis added] servant to the lender" and sometimes servant to the lender's enforcement agency, the court. This kind of servitude always disgraces the cause of Christ. The understanding that debt is a type of slavery lends support to Ryrie's bold assertion that "debt is to be abhorred as much as slavery."[36] Indeed, debt is as potentially degrading as slavery.

---

[33] George Lawson, *Exposition of Proverbs* (1829; repr., Grand Rapids: Kregel Publications, 1980), 589.

[34] Charles C. Ryrie says they are synonymous ideas. "Owe a Man? Oh No, Man!" *Moody Monthly*, March, 1979, 36. However, the loosing may not denote release from slavery, but simply a loosing from obligation and from the possibility of arrest. Broadus, 391.

[35] See, for example, Matt. 27:15; Luke 23:22; John 19:10; Acts 16:35; and 26:32. In all these verses ἀπολύω means to let a captive go free.

[36] Ryrie, 36.

Debt Burden

The debtor not only enslaves himself, he also places himself under a heavy burden, for the Scriptures consistently speak of debt as a burdensome misfortune.[37] In biblical times the poor man, not the rich man, borrowed money or goods. Therefore, the one who needed to borrow was the least able to pay back the loan. Debt placed the man burdened with poverty under the greater burden of debt. Despite the fact that some definitions of debt in today's world are euphemized (e.g., a "second mortgage" is much easier to market as "equity access"), the "debt" entry from Roget's Thesaurus clearly suggests how onerous and burdensome debt actually is: obligation, liability, bill, debit, arrears, deficit, pledge, due, burden, red ink.[38]

Although several Old Testament passages teach that the debtor was most likely a poor man, the mention of one will suffice. Moses instructed the Israelites,

> And if thy brother be waxen poor, and fallen in decay with thee; then thou shalt relieve him: yea, though he be a stranger, or a sojourner; that he may live with thee. Take thou no usury of him, or increase: but fear thy God; that thy brother may live with thee. Thou shalt not give him thy money upon usury, nor lend him thy victuals for increase (Lev. 25:35–37).[39]

When an Israelite became poor and unable to sustain his family, the more prosperous Israelite was figuratively to "take him by

---

[37] W. H. Bennett, "Debt, Debtor," *A Dictionary of the Bible*, ed. James Hastings (New York: Charles Scribner's Sons, 1898), 1:579. Some of the most pertinent passages are Exod. 22:25; Deut. 15:7–11; 24:6, 17; 2 Kings 4:1–7; and Luke 7:41–42.

[38] Marc McCutcheon, *Roget's Super Thesaurus* (Cincinnati: Writer's Digest Books, 1995), 137.

[39] Cf. Exod. 22:25; Deut. 15:7–8; and 24:10–12. See also 1 Sam. 22:2.

the arm" to "relieve" him in his misfortune.[40] That the poor man might have to borrow money was burden enough. To insure that the lender did not add burden to burden, the Lord forbade interest charges on money or food. Kellogg has aptly summed up the onus of debt's entanglements for a poor man: "Debt is a burden in any case, to a poor man especially; but debt is the heavier burden when to the original debt is added the constant payment of interest."[41] Having to pay a high interest rate is the condition in which a debtor would almost certainly find himself in today's society. The average APR on a new credit card in America in 2009 was 14.23 percent.[42]

The New Testament also describes debt as a burden. Illustrating the magnitude of God's forgiveness, Jesus incidentally portrayed the burdensomeness of debt. A short parable in Luke 7:41–42 depicts two men in debt: one owed five hundred pence, the other fifty.[43] The one having the greater burden of debt appreciated release from the burden more than his counterpart. No doubt Christ chose debtors for His parabolic characters because His contemporaries readily recognized debt as burdensome. As one esteems financial liberty in proportion to the amount of debt cancelled, so one loves God in proportion to the estimation of one's pardoned sin-debt. Great relief comes to the one who escapes either load. As Charles Spurgeon has said, "Without debt, without care; out of debt, out of danger."[44]

---

[40] *KD, Pentateuch*, 2:464.

[41] Kellogg, *The Book of Leviticus*, 496.

[42] http://www.creditcards.com/credit-card-news/credit-card-industry-facts-personal-debt-statistics-1276.php.

[43] The Greek word for "pence" means "denarii." The Roman denarius was a good wage for a day's work. Therefore, the greater debtor owed more than a year's wages.

[44] Charles Haddon Spurgeon, *John Ploughman's Talks* (Chicago: Moody Press, n.d.), 60.

In summary, the Bible portrays debt as a burden for anyone, but especially for those least able to bear it and yet most likely to suffer it. One of the poor man's greatest joys was to get out of debt. The Bible parallels financial debt with the greatest of all debts, the debt of sin. The effect of release from the former illustrates the loving gratitude effected by release from the latter. Considering the seriousness of debt, one could hardly be overcautious to shoulder its burden.

The Impropriety of Suretyship

Suretyship, the assumption of responsibility for debts in the event of another's default, can obligate a surety beyond his ability to pay.[45] Of course, a person need not become surety for another in the first place. But even if he carefully undertakes the obligation and initially has the means to cover the default, the guarantor has no assurance that his assets will remain the same or that the debtor's financial condition will not worsen. Because of the potential dangers of suretyship, the Scriptures portray it as something to avoid.[46]

Proverbs is replete with instruction about suretyship. Proverbs 6:1–5 exhorts the guarantor to free himself from the obligation at all costs. According to Solomon's illustration, suretyship is inadvisable in every way, for the guarantor has been "snared" and

---

[45] Roland de Vaux defines suretyship more technically: "In biblical law the surety is the person who, when the debt matures, 'intervenes' (the root 'rb), in favour of the solvent debtor and assumes responsibility for the payment of the debt, either by obtaining it from the debtor or by substituting himself for him." *Ancient Israel*, 172.

[46] There are a few seeming exceptions. Reuben and Judah became surety for Benjamin (Gen. 42:37; 43:9; 44:32–33). But they were pledging their lives rather than their money. Paul presents a possible exception. He offered to become the financial surety for Onesimus (Philem. 18, 19). However, Paul's reminder to Philemon that he owed Paul a spiritual debt (v. 19) strongly suggests that Paul did not expect Philemon to press for the payment. See Jac. J. Müller, *The Epistles of Paul to the Philippians and to Philemon*, 188, and Herbert M. Carson, *The Epistles of Paul to the Colossians and Philemon* (Grand Rapids: Eerdmans, 1979), 111.

"trapped" (v. 2, KJV "taken") by his words of promise.[47] The figure of verse two comes from hunting—"the unwary surety is an animal caught in a trap."[48] His predicament is so dire that he should "deliver" himself immediately by placing himself in a position of humility before his friend, by impetuously assailing his friend to fulfill his obligation,[49] and by taking no rest until the friend has done just that. As this passage suggests, suretyship is particularly unwise when one enters it rashly, without carefully weighing its benefits against its baneful effects.[50] But it is also unwise because it makes one liable into the uncertain future and because it places the surety at the mercy of both the creditor and debtor. Even the debtor, who ought to be the one in danger, has his surety in a tempting position. That is, by defaulting, the debtor can escape his debt and leave his surety in the lurch. Of course, the conscientious debtor would never default if he could help it, but unavoidable circumstances could cause him to default in spite of his best intentions.

"He who is guarantor for a stranger will surely suffer for it, but he who hates being a guarantor is secure" (11:15, NASB). This warning against suretyship adds another caution. Previous verses portrayed the guarantor as helping a "friend" (6:1), but here he helps a "stranger." Obligating oneself for a stranger with unknown character is bound to "smart" (KJV).[51] The best policy is no longer

---

[47] Crawford H. Toy suggests "trapped" as the best translation for לכד. *Proverbs*, 119. See also *TWOT*, 1:480.

[48] Toy, 120. Verse five makes the hunting figure obvious—"Deliver thyself as a roe from the hand of the hunter, and as a bird from the hand of the fowler."

[49] See *KD*, *Proverbs*, 1:136, for "humble thyself" (v. 3).

[50] The statement "Thou art snared with the words of thy mouth, thou art taken with the words of thy mouth" suggests that the guarantor made a rash commitment. The guarantor obligated himself with a verbal promise without seriously considering all the ramifications. See Bridges, *Proverbs*, 60.

[51] The Hebrew idiom רע ירוע suggests that the guarantor suffers a grave injustice. He will indeed smart because he is "badly treated (maltreated) in a bad way." *KD*,

release from obligation but avoidance of it altogether. One who hates suretyship, who despises it and keeps his distance from it,[52] will have a feeling of financial safety and security.[53]

The next indictment against suretyship is 17:18: "A man void of understanding striketh hands, and becometh surety in the presence of his friend."[54] The man who pledges to pay another's debts is "lacking in sense" (NASB). While appearing to manifest a kind spirit, a man may actually evince intellectual ineptness. This lack of sense or wisdom typifies not only a man who errs financially, but one who commits adultery (6:32), deserves the rod of punishment (10:13), despises his neighbor (11:12), pursues worthless things (12:11), rejoices over foolishness (15:21), is slothful (24:30–31), and oppresses when in authority (28:16).[55] By implication, then, one who would become a surety may lack moral uprightness, love for others, diligence, and a proper estimation of the true values of life.

Speaking contemptuously, Solomon continues the warnings about suretyship: "Take his garment that is surety for a stranger: and take a pledge of him for a strange woman" (20:16).[56] The one foolish enough to become surety for a stranger, or worse for a "strange woman," ought to pay the legal penalty.[57] Suretyship is an unwise and unfair obligation, but one imprudent enough to undertake it needs to learn from experience his foolishness.

Proverbs, 1:238.

[52] See *TWOT*'s discussion of the root meaning of "to hate." 2:880.

[53] *TWOT*, 1:101 shows that the root word for "safe" ("sure," KJV) emphasizes the "feeling of being safe or secure."

[54] The striking of hands (similar to shaking hands today) between guarantor and creditor ratified the agreement. This was the legal procedure for concluding an agreement (cf. 2 Kings 10:15). Toy, 121.

[55] In all these verses, excluding 28:16, which uses similar terminology, Solomon employs the Hebrew idiom חֲסַר לֵב (lit., "he is lacking heart") to describe this man.

[56] Cf. 27:13.

[57] Possibly the term "strange woman" designated a prostitute. *KD, Proverbs*, 2:50. Cf. 5:20; 6:24; and 7:5. Toy, 309.

Of all the references, the last one shows most clearly how debt and suretyship can unfairly obligate others. First the writer forbids suretyship: "Be not thou one of them that strike hands, or of them that are sureties for debts" (22:26). Then he explains why it is foolish: "If thou hast nothing to pay, why should he take away thy bed from under thee?" (22:27). A debtor can obligate his surety friend to the point that the friend loses his last piece of furniture—an unfair obligation by any standard.

We have learned that any debt is especially unwise when it unfairly obligates others. This unfair liability occurs when one procures either friend or stranger as a surety for a debt. Neither the debtor nor the surety can foresee his future financial status. Therefore, both the debtor and the surety would benefit by avoiding the surety relationship altogether. Although Paul's example with Philemon may be an exception, the rule is certainly that found in Proverbs. Proverbs strictly forbids suretyship and by implication the debt that makes it necessary. Every prospective debtor should ponder the thought that though he be solvent at present, he knows not whether he will be richer or poorer at the day of payment.[58] The uncertainties of the future make debt and suretyship a very risky business.[59]

Jeopardizing Family Security

2 Kings 4:1–7 furnishes the first example of the potential of debt to destroy family security. The two sons of the prophet were headed for enslavement, and family security was thus in jeopardy.[60] The account does not describe how the children's father, a

---

[58] Lawson, 611.

[59] Larry Burkett warns pastors that "almost half of the people who co-sign loans are ultimately asked to pay for them." "Legal Guide," *Church Business Report*, December 1981, 3.

[60] The Mosaic Law authorized this type of bondage for the time remaining until the year of Jubilee (Lev. 25:40).

man of God and peer of Elisha, got into debt. Whether because of Jezebel's persecution, unforeseen difficulties, or even his own imprudence, this man who feared God had fallen upon hard times. Actually he may not have contracted debt at all. Instead, because of her destitution, his widow may have pledged the services of her two sons as security for a loan to buy food and other necessities.[61] But whether husband or wife contracted the debt is immaterial. The point is clear that debt had jeopardized the family's security and future. Without divine intervention on her behalf, the mother could expect years of paying off the family's debts, and the sons could expect years of servitude. The widow, like most debtors in her day, was poor and had virtually no alternative to borrowing money. Poverty produced debt, and debt produced more poverty. The cycle was vicious, and she was now caught in it.

Elisha did not censure the widow's creditors, for they evidently were following Mosaic Law (Lev. 25:39–40), but Nehemiah censured the creditors of his day (Neh. 5) because they were usurious of each other and thus in violation of the Law (Lev. 25:35–37). He stopped the rich creditors from exploiting the poor with usurious loans.[62] The situation had reached emergency status. Whole families were facing imminent starvation, having already borrowed and mortgaged themselves to the hilt. So deep in debt were some families that they sold their sons and daughters as servants (5:5). That they sold their daughters into bondage, a practice that only the worst of hardships could occasion, illustrates how seriously debt can jeopardize a family's future.[63]

---

[61] Ronald S. Wallace, *Elijah and Elisha* (Grand Rapids: Eerdmans, 1957), 100.

[62] Nehemiah was not condemning loans per se, for he himself had loaned to the poor ("And likewise I, my brothers and my servants, are lending them money and grain," 5:10*a*, NASB). Rather, he was condemning the charging of interest on the loans ("Please, let us leave off this usury," 5:10*b*, NASB).

[63] *KD, Ezra, Nehemiah, Esther*, 209.

A debtor in biblical times could lose his material goods as well as the services of his children.[64] Proverbs 22:27 says, "If thou hast nothing to pay, why should he take away thy bed from under thee?" A beleaguered debtor could lose everything he owned. Of course, one whose debt had reached great proportions and protraction could expect such extreme measures from his creditors.[65] Debtors could not count on compassion, especially when they had obligated themselves foolishly.[66] They could jeopardize their family's security with excessive indebtedness, for even the family's last item of furniture was not exempt from the exacting creditor.[67]

In the parable of the unmerciful slave (Matt. 18:23–35), Jesus further described the result of large indebtedness. In this case the creditor demanded that not only the debtor be sold, but also "his wife and children, and all that he had" (18:25). Although the creditor's intention sounds outrageous, the above discussion has shown its plausibility.

All of the verses we have considered demonstrate clearly that debt can be a canker upon the family's future. A family may have to forfeit its furniture, or worse, its children, to the possession and service of the creditor. Although many Americans do not seem to realize the destructive potential of debt for their families and descendants, a day of reckoning is coming. What is true within the family is also true nationally; debt must be paid, and if this generation does not pay it, its descendants must. The brouhaha in 2010 over Greece's inability to pay its national debt and the

---

[64] Technically, in the suretyship relation there are both a debtor and a surety for the debtor. Recall the definition of suretyship under "The Impropriety of Suretyship." The surety is in view here, but he becomes a debtor when the original debtor defaults.

[65] Cf. Prov. 20:16.

[66] Note the injunction here against becoming a surety (22:26).

[67] The Lord does not approve of such harsh exactions. See Exod. 22:26–27; Deut. 24:6, 13; Job 22:5–6; and 24:3. America's current bankruptcy laws are generally much less severe to debtors.

ongoing rumblings for other similarly indebted nations (including the USA!) are the tip of the iceberg of what could happen to any people living beyond their means.

Debt that imperils one's family and posterity is unwise biblically, but also ethically. As Otto Piper rightly deduces,

> The harmony of the economic society requires that debts and loans be paid back in the lifetime of those who have borrowed, and to their full original value. It is utterly unethical to make our children or grandchildren pay the cost of benefits which we enjoy when we were in a position to pay for them.[68]

This kind of integrity is becoming almost passé in our day of entitlement without a sense of responsibility. Radio advertisements even offer to help the debtor get out of his obligations by paying only a fraction of what he owes. Debtors without integrity may like that appeal, but honorable creditors will be robbed in the process. Bankruptcy laws vary considerably from state to state, but the fact is that bankruptcy in America will often exempt such things as clothes, household items, trade tools, books, Social Security payments, unemployment insurance and even some equity in homes.

Bondage or Imprisonment

Previous treatment has shown that debt places one in the role of a servant and under a burden. Financial servitude and bondage is bad enough, but the debtor can face even worse consequences—physical bondage or imprisonment. Moses warned that an Israelite might face slavery because of his indebtedness: "If a countryman of yours becomes so poor with regard to you that he sells himself to you, you shall not subject him to a slave's service" (Lev.

---

[68] Otto A. Piper, *The Christian Meaning of Money* (Englewood Cliffs, NJ: Prentice-Hall, 1965), 103.

25:39,NASB). Having to sell oneself into slavery was a last resort, but it could happen.[69] Moses was not forbidding the practice; he was forbidding the harsh treatment of the enslaved debtor.[70] The proposed bondage was actually humane, for it was an honorable way for the debtor to work off his debt directly.[71]

In Matthew 5:25–26 (cf. Luke 12:58–59) Jesus used the imprisonment of debtors as the basis for spiritual instruction. Apparently creditors in Christ's day commonly used legal avenues to exact payment from debtors. They brought debtors before a judge, who then sentenced them to imprisonment until they became solvent. Jesus compares this practice with God's exaction of the sinner's debt to divine justice. As surely as a debtor will face imprisonment, the unforgiving sinner will face God's judgment. The key element for this discussion is the normal consequence of unresolved debt—imprisonment. Jesus recommends quick and effective action by the debtor: "Make friends quickly with your opponent at law while you are with him on the way" (5:25a, NASB). A concerted and determined effort at solvency is far better than the debtor's prison.

Christ further portrays the predicament of the debtor in the parable of the unmerciful servant (Matt. 18:23–35). Some creditors dealt violently with debtors: "But that slave went out and found

---

[69] The citation by George Bush of the Jewish writer Maimonides suggests that a Jew's selling himself into slavery was a last resort: "A man might not sell himself to lay up the money which was given for him; nor to buy goods; nor to pay his debts, but merely that he might get bread to eat. Neither was it lawful for him to sell himself as long as he had so much as a garment left." *Notes, Critical and Practical on the Book of Leviticus* (1852; repr., Minneapolis: Klock and Klock, 1979), 260. Although slavery was a last resort, it did occur. See Exod. 21:2.

[70] Gordon J. Wenham translates the last phrase, "Do not boss him around harshly." *The Book of Leviticus* (Grand Rapids: Eerdmans, 1979), 322.

[71] Ibid. Enslavement by one Hebrew of another Hebrew was humane in other ways also. It could last only six years unless the slave voluntarily wished to continue it (Exod. 21:2). Then, too, the slave's relatives had an option to buy him in order to set him free (Lev. 25:47–54).

one of his fellow slaves who owed him a hundred denarii; and he seized him and began to choke him" (18:28, NASB). Also, some creditors took matters in their own hands, personally "casting" debtors into prison.[72] But the worst that could happen to the debtor was to face the "tormentors" (18:34).[73] These officials, appointed by the courts to torture the worst offenders, used methods such as cumbering prisoners with heavy chains, near-starvation rationing, protracted labor, and bodily tortures.[74] This unpleasant picture of the legal consequences of debt in Bible times serves as a stern caution against it.

Presumption upon the Future

Solomon's words "Boast not thyself of to morrow; for thou knowest not what a day may bring forth" (Prov. 27:1) apply to the prospective borrower. In discussing the "spiritual dangers of debt," Christian writer Ron Blue asserts that "borrowing always presumes upon the future."[75] One who borrows money plans to pay the loan back; otherwise he is stealing rather than borrowing, for the Bible characterizes the dishonest borrower as wicked: "The wicked borroweth, and payeth not again" (Ps. 37:21a). But assuming that the borrower plans to pay back his loan, he must still recognize that the future is uncertain. Since the honest debtor borrows only what he thinks he can pay back in a reasonable amount of time, before borrowing he will try to figure his income and how long it will

---

[72] Adolf Deissman has found that this system of "personal execution by imprisonment for debt" was widespread in Graeco-Roman lands. *Light from the Ancient East*, trans. Lionel R. M. Strachan, 4th ed. (New York: Harper and Brothers, [1927]), 270. But William Hendriksen thinks the expression "he threw him in jail" is simply idiomatic for "he had him jailed." *New Testament Commentary: Exposition of the Gospel According to Matthew* (Grand Rapids: Baker, 1973), 707.

[73] The noun βασανιστής occurs only here in the New Testament. However, see Rev. 9:5 and 18:7 (where the verb βασανίζω and the noun βασανισμός respectively are used) to get some idea of the horrible pain implied by the word.

[74] Hendricksen, 709; Lenski, *St. Matthew's Gospel*, 723.

[75] Blue, 68.

take him to pay back the loan. However, this projection of future income is dubious, because it presumes upon an uncertain future. This presumption may fall under Solomon's as well as James's condemnation of arrogant overconfidence. James describes the businessman's presumption upon the future as "boastings," and "evil" boastings at that (4:16). "An impious and empty presumption which trusts in the stability of earthly things is wicked."[76] The remedy for this presumption is a humble acknowledgement of and trust in God's sovereign control of circumstances (4:15). Today's real-estate market illustrates how easily people fall into this trap of presuming upon the future appreciation of their assets. According to an online *Wall Street Journal* article dated November 24, 2009, "the proportion of U.S. homeowners who owe more on their mortgages than the properties are worth has swelled to about 23%."[77] How many of these people thought their homes would decline in value and would decline to less than they had paid for them?

Now is an appropriate time to return to a text already considered under suretyship and to note its warning about the extreme danger of presumption. Solomon admonished his son, "Do not be among those who give pledges, among those who become guarantors for debts. If you have nothing with which to pay, why should he take your bed from under you?" (Prov. 22:26–27, NASB). "If" indicates a very real possibility, a situation where the son will not have the means to pay. Waltke explains the sage's reasoning: "Although at the time of becoming the surety he may have had the financial means to risk becoming guarantor, future financial reversals may expose him to losing everything he owns."[78]

---

[76] Thayer, 24.

[77] http://online.wsj.com/article/SB125903489722661849.html.

[78] Bruce Waltke, *The Book of Proverbs: Chapters 15–31*, in *The New International Commentary on the Old Testament* (Grand Rapids: Eerdmans, 2005), 234.

In light of these dangers and uncertainties, some will no doubt wonder whether a debt such as a home mortgage is ever acceptable. Obviously any debt can be risky, but remember that by one definition debt is inability to honor the contract for which one has engaged. Therefore, one with reasonable assurance that he can make his payments may legitimately decide that taking a loan on such an item that normally appreciates is better stewardship of his funds than renting. However, almost all economists would point out that even apart from scriptural warnings, debt on depreciating items (e.g., cars, appliances, furniture) is unwise. Popular speaker and writer Dave Ramsey says this about such debt: "If you must borrow money, let me give you two basic guidelines. First, borrow on short terms and only borrow on items that go up in value. That means never on anything except possibly a home, which you should pay off as soon as possible."[79] Some might not go as far as Ramsey and might make allowance for borrowing on something as necessary as a car, but even then limited borrowing is the wiser use of money.

Not only individuals but churches also ignore this caution against presumptuous indebtedness. Some have gone into large bond programs because they have projected a church growth that would theoretically take care of the indebtedness. These projections are precarious at best and may also fall under James's censure of evil boastings.[80]

---

[79] Dave Ramsey, *Financial Peace* (New York: Viking Penguin, 1997), 87.

[80] Lyle E. Schaller calls these projections "architectural evangelism." This projection assumes that a beautiful new building will attract the new members needed to pay for it. But the projection is presumptuous and often faulty. As Schaller warns, "Do not depend on it to pay off the mortgage!" "Guidelines for Borrowing for a Building Program: How Much Should We Borrow," *Church Management: The Clergy Journal*, LV (October, 1978), 20.

The Bible clearly mandates the attitude that the Christian should have toward the future. He must never forget that he does not know the future accurately and certainly, and that human life is transitory and insecure.[81] Therefore, the Christian must prudently consider the uncertainties of the future before going into debt. To do otherwise is to presume wickedly upon God.

Worldly Philosophy

The world's philosophy focuses on pleasure and urges us to enjoy now and pay later. Greed and covetousness help fuel the practice of this philosophy. As psychiatrist Edward J. Khantzian of the Harvard Medical School has observed concerning the indebtedness of many Americans, "It all boils down to the inability to accept limits."[82] Thus easy credit has enticed many Americans, including Christians, to enjoy conveniences and luxuries for which they cannot pay. Targeted ads have inured Americans to debt's hazards. "What has been deliberately and socially acceptable was not too long ago thought to be irresponsible both financially and morally."[83] Although the Bible cautions against this philosophy, many Christians are feeling the yoke of debt because they are ignoring the biblical injunctions.

In contrast to hedonism, the philosophy of Scripture calls for man to deny himself. In fact, man's demand for indulging his flesh is the very thing that brings God's judgment. For example, having listed a number of the "works of the flesh," the "results of surrender"

---

[81] See Prov. 27:1 and James 4:14. Stewart Custer points out that "know" in James 4:14 means to "know accurately." *A Treasury of New Testament Synonyms* (Greenville: Bob Jones University Press, 1975), 112. Thus James implies that no one knows the future accurately or certainly.

[82] Quoted in Otto Friedrich, "The American Way of Debt," *Time*, May 31, 1981, 47.

[83] Jim Wallis, *Rediscovering Values* (New York: Howard Books, 2010), 48. Wallis pushes a social-justice agenda, often to the ignoring of cardinal Bible doctrines, but on the matter of debt his observation hits home.

to the desires of the flesh,[84] Paul warns about those "works" when he writes, "of the which I tell you before, as I have also told you in time past, that they which do such things shall not inherit the kingdom of God" (Gal. 5:21). In another place, again listing some of the same works of the flesh, Paul states explicitly that God pours out His wrath on the "children of disobedience" who practice those things.[85]

Jesus also demanded that His followers discipline themselves. He said, "If any man will come after me, let him deny himself, and take up his cross, and follow me" (Matt. 16:24). One must be disciplined enough to die for Christ's sake if necessary. Should not then the believer discipline himself when he goes to buy a sofa or a car?

Solomon, too, warned of the worldly philosophy of hedonism that seeks to enjoy life now and disregard the future. He affirmed, "He that loveth pleasure shall be a poor man: he that loveth wine and oil shall not be rich" (Prov. 21:17). Unbridled luxurious living usually leads to excessive spending. Those who must have the "dainties" now will come to want the necessities later.[86] Thus Solomon implicitly warns against credit buying. He implies that some hardship and denial is far better than ultimate, degrading poverty. Ironically, the "person who chases after the pleasures of life comes only to lack what is desirable and necessary to life."[87]

Covetousness helps fuel the natural tendency to "sacrifice" thriftiness on the "altar" of self-gratification. Covetousness is idolatry

---

[84] Joseph Agar Beet, *Commentary on St. Paul's Epistle to the Galatians* (London: Hodder and Stoughton, 1903), 157.

[85] Col. 3:6. Cf. Eph. 5:3–6.

[86] Bridges, 380.

[87] Waltke, *The Book of Proverbs: Chapters 15–31*, 181.

(Col. 3:5) and can lead to enslavement to debt.[88] Paul's observations no doubt aptly describe many today who have fallen into the credit trap:

> But they that will be rich ["want to get rich," NASB] fall into temptation and a snare, and into many foolish and hurtful lusts, which drown men in destruction and perdition. For the love of money is the root of all evil: which while some coveted after, they have erred from the faith, and pierced themselves through with many sorrows (1 Tim. 6:9–10).

In today's easy-credit society, one can easily indulge a love for the things that borrowed money can buy. That is, at least for a time, a person can live as one "wanting to get rich" whether he is truly financially rich or not. However, the consequences of indulgent living are far more unpleasant than one used to affluence might expect: "destruction," "perdition," a straying away from the faith, and "many sorrows."

In summary, Christians must guard against the world's philosophy on debt. Years ago, even the public consensus frowned upon borrowing and lending. "To our colonial ancestors," Newman and Kramer write, "money-lending seemed a dubious occupation, on the respectability scale falling somewhere between witchcraft and highway robbery."[89] But that attitude clearly does not prevail today. Americans have generally fallen prey to a philosophy of enjoy now and pay later. This philosophy contradicts the biblical injunction to avoid indulgence and covetousness. Then, too, debt often breaks down the self-discipline so necessary for Christian

---

[88] Cf. Eph. 5:5, where the covetous man is also called an idolater.

[89] Stephen A. Newman and Nancy Kramer, "Getting All You Deserve," *The Christian Home*, March–May 1981, 24.

character development.[90] Therefore, the Christian must learn contentment with "such things" as he has (Heb. 13:5), especially when the purchase of other things may erode discipline and encourage indulgence. Surely he does not want the "destruction" and "many sorrows" Paul warns about.

The Liability Principle

The Bible states unequivocally that "the wicked borroweth, and payeth not again" (Ps. 37:21). This delinquency in payment is a common abuse arising from debt. Because a debtor is already in financial straits, he tends to renege on his obligation to his creditors. All borrowers face that temptation, and many succumb. Because of the current decline in housing values and the large number of borrowers who are "underwater" (the value of the house is less than the amount owed), a new "strategy" for dealing with the problem has become popular. This new scheme is called "strategic defaults." These accounted for 12 percent of defaults in February 2010. An article in *Bloomberg Business Week* explains: "A homeowner in that position may decide that continuing to make payments is throwing money away, or may default to get the lender to modify the loan."[91] Such action is clearly unethical. Unless the debtor is using bankruptcy simply as a means for getting time to set his financial house in order and pay off his creditors in full, both strategic defaults and bankruptcy are dishonorable for the Christian. They amount to a broken agreement with his creditors. Ethically the debt is still there, and for the sake of the gospel the Christian must make every effort to satisfy the debt even after bankruptcy. The tendency of debt to grow, the various ways to avoid repaying debts in full, and the relatively soft bankruptcy laws can easily lead a

---

[90] Crawford, *A Christian and His Money*, 96.

[91] Jody Shenn, "Strategic Defaults Are on the Rise," *Bloomberg Business Week*, May 10–16, 2010, 45–46.

Christian down the road of credit abuse. Not only is one who re-neges on his debts a thief and "wicked" (Ps. 37:21), but he is also a liability to others. Irresponsible debtors cost other Americans billions of dollars, because someone must pay. Usually the other consumers pay through higher prices, higher interest rates, and tighter credit.[92]

Borrowers have too often abused their privilege. Some had good intentions when they borrowed, but unforeseen circumstances made them unable to repay. Others had only halfhearted intentions to repay or even high hopes for turning a quick profit by "flipping" their property. Whatever the case, many borrowers have not adequately considered the caution that debt is liable to intentional and unintentional abuse. Easy credit has enticed many into debt, and the dilating bankruptcy escape has offered a seemingly acceptable way to walk away from it. Because of the groundswell of debt, today's Christian must give special heed to the biblical cautions.

PRACTICAL CAUTIONS

The biblical cautions against debt are common-sense cautions, for the Bible is a practical book. Nevertheless, there are some other practical cautions based on sound economics and on discerning observations of the effects of debt.

Hidden Costs

Making money by borrowing money is possible in today's economy, and some dealers in real estate have capitalized on it. One went so far as to say that

> the secret of making real estate pay is borrowing. The idea
> of assuming what may seem a staggering debt flies in the

---

[92] Bob Whitmore, "Bankruptcy." *Faith for the Family*, November, 1981, 12.

face of conventional wisdom. Yet borrowing is the only means most people have of acquiring real estate—and it is the shortest route to high returns.[93]

But he is only partially correct. He has omitted the fact that nothing, including real estate, is sure to appreciate.[94] Moreover, although the purchase of real estate may turn out to be a good investment, the truth about borrowing is that it almost always costs more.[95] Borrowers often pay back over twice the value of the original loan. Such borrowing is often poor stewardship.

Hindering Effects

Indebtedness has hindered many Christian laymen and many prospective missionaries and Christian workers from doing God's will. Charles C. Ryrie, a seminary professor, told of one man who wanted to prepare for Christian service but who could not because he had too many debts from buying professional equipment, an expensive house, and two new cars.[96] Relating his experiences to aspiring preachers, Ryrie claimed,

> I have seen seminary students hampered by debts they have incurred in buying expensive cars, by wanting the latest clothes, or best housing, and costly entertainment. The slavery of these debts binds them to extra hours on the job, to having their wives work and their homes affected, to poorer grades than normal, to missed opportunities for summer ministries.[97]

---

[93] Samuel A. Schreiner, Jr., "Beat Inflation—With Real Estate," *Reader's Digest*, March 1981, 140.

[94] Ryrie, 37.

[95] Crawford, 96.

[96] Ryrie, 36.

[97] Ibid.

That many Christian workers have foolishly limited their availability because of debt is tragic.

Debt can also hinder an individual from giving freely and liberally to the Lord's work. A Christian in debt has an obligation to his creditors. This monthly obligation automatically limits that Christian's financial liberty in giving.

Debt Escalation

Debt, once indulged, has a tendency to increase. For instance, the national debt on July 4, 2000, was $5.65 trillion. Only ten years later, on July 4, 2010, it was almost $13.2 trillion.[98] It has more than doubled in only ten years! A recent report about the nation's debt substantiates this assertion. From 1971 to 1981, governmental (federal, state, and local) debts increased 137 percent.[99] This snowballing effect happened, in part, because people have treated symptoms rather than causes.

Some have assumed that a loan consolidation would solve their problems. This approach is appealing because it reduces a borrower's creditors from several down to one. However, it may produce a false sense of security and lead to more debts because the borrower has not dealt with his root problem—a tendency to live beyond his means. In answer to the question, "How do you feel about transferring balances between credit cards?" financial advisors Richard Baland and A. H. Barbee write, "Pay them off or reduce them. Transferring accomplishes nothing. Let us not confuse activity with progress."[100]

---

[98] http://www.treasurydirect.gov/NP/NPGateway.

[99] "Who Owes the Nation's $5 Trillion Debt," *U.S. News and World Report*, January 25, 1982, 38.

[100] Richard Baland and A. H. Barbee, *Christians and Their Money* (n.p.: n.p., 2006), 142.

The tendency of debt to escalate compounds because those who borrow are also those most likely to have bad spending habits. Because credit is easily gotten, those used to buying on credit often drown themselves in debt before they know they are in deep water.[101] "Debts and sins are more than we think them," said Spurgeon. "They accumulate insensibly, and we are willing to forget them."[102]

CONCLUSION

Some godly men have believed that even the smallest debt constitutes excessive indebtedness. George Müller stated frankly, "As regards borrowing money, I have considered that there is no ground to go away from the door of the Lord to that of a believer, so long as He is willing to supply the need."[103] He also believed that "the incurring of debt, being unscriptural, is a sin needing confession and abandonment if we desire unhindered fellowship."[104] Charles Spurgeon would have agreed: "Scripture says, 'Owe no man anything,' which does not mean pay your debts, but never have any to pay."[105]

Although Müller and Spurgeon did live in economic times different from today's, one contesting their view about debt must adequately explain Romans 13:8. The first half of the verse literally reads, "Owe nothing to anyone except to love one another" (NASB). The obvious and broadest meaning is that the Christian should have no debt of any kind, whether monetary or ethical,

---

[101] As one writer puts it, "Perhaps the most striking fact about almost every debtor in real trouble is that he has no idea how much he owes—much less what exorbitant interest he is usually paying." Friedrich, 49.

[102] Charles Haddon Spurgeon, *Spurgeon's Proverbs and Sayings with Notes* (repr., Grand Rapids: Baker, 1975), 1:117.

[103] Pierson, *George Müller of Bristol*, 454.

[104] Ibid., 176.

[105] *John Ploughman's Talks*, 60.

other than the ongoing debt of love. Although one must constantly pay on the debt of love, one can never pay that debt in full.[106] We have already learned that debt is not always forbidden, so we should also understand Paul's words not to forbid debt absolutely. However, these words at the least require the believer to meet every obligation he has. They also certainly suggest that no financial indebtedness of any kind is the Christian's ideal.[107]

Even though Christ suggested that there would be those who legitimately need to borrow money (Matt. 5:42; Luke 6:34–35), He never encouraged borrowing money. Coupled with Romans 13:8, the biblical and practical cautions against debt make it a perilous practice. By ignoring any one of the cautions, a person will have excessive indebtedness. Such indebtedness can be a hindrance to, or worse, the decline of, one's spiritual fervor, effectiveness, and availability. Christians need to get back to the biblical concept of debt. A loan can help a Christian in dire need, but excessive debt can destroy a Christian's usefulness. Debt can bring temporary relief, but it can also bring untold distress. The Christian may legitimately borrow money, but he must do so only after heeding the biblical and practical cautions, while always aiming for the ideal of owing "no man any thing" (Rom. 13:8).

I will close this chapter with anecdotal evidence of the need for such a chapter. After spending an afternoon making some final corrections to this book, I was listening to the news on NPR. The commentator was explaining that the United States is now indebted to China for well over $1 trillion. (China owns that many

---

[106] Malcolm MacGregor and Stanley C. Baldwin, *Your Money Matters* (Minneapolis: Bethany Fellowship, 1977), 11–12.

[107] Admittedly Paul envisioned more than financial debt. However, the immediate context is partially monetary in focus. In verse 6 Paul mentions the payment of "tribute" (taxes upon houses, lands, and persons, Thayer, 657), and in verse 7 he adds the payment of "custom," which is an indirect tax on goods.

of our treasury bonds.) He said there was both good news and bad news regarding this. The bad news is that China could destroy our economy if it demanded repayment (by selling the bonds) on a large portion of the bonds. The "good" news is that doing so would destroy China's own economy in the process. He called this "mutual assured economic destruction." This is *not* good news, no matter how it is presented. As individuals we can do relatively little about how those in power handle our national finances, but we can have much control over our personal finances. Let us be zealous to avoid being any man's slave through debt.

6

CAPITALISM OR SOCIALISM?

Since the US presidential election of 2008 and the express intention of some of the president's policies to expand government and redistribute wealth, the term *socialism* has been very much in the public discourse. Adding to the assault on the *free enterprise system*[1] by liberalism are the criticisms leveled even by evangelicals. Some of these writers have strongly condemned the free enterprise system of economics and the resulting distribution of wealth in the world. Some even go so far as to equate categorically a high standard of living with injustice to those with less wealth. For example, Jim Wallis, editor of the social- and environmental-activist magazine *Sojourners*, claims that "our standard of living is rooted in injustice. Our hope is others' despair; our good life perpetuates their misery."[2] Similarly, Ronald Sider, corresponding editor for *Christianity Today* and president of Evangelicals for Social Action, says, "Left to itself, a market-driven economy will simply supply what the wealthy can pay for—even if millions of poor folk starve."[3] Even more recently, theologian Dewi Hughes has charged that "the way we live in luxury in the minority world while millions die in poverty could well make us liable for the blood of the poor before God. Ignorance and a lack of intent can reduce

---

[1] The critics of capitalism do not like this designation of it because it emphasizes not the presumably corrupt and oppressive "free market" but the freedom of hard work and ingenuity of the workers.

[2] Wallis, *The Call to Conversion*, 46.

[3] Ronald J. Sider, *Rich Christians in an Age of Hunger*, 5th ed. (Nashville: Thomas Nelson, 2005), 138.

culpability, but there could still be blood on our hands."[4] The answer to the problem of the poor? Sider's proposal is the redistribution of wealth: "If we start with the present division of wealth, the outcome of the market will be ghastly injustice. Only if redistribution occurs—through private and/or public measures—will the poorest obtain the capital to earn a decent living in the global market."[5] Note that Sider is not talking primarily about private charity but rather about government control ("public measures"). He believes that government must take action: "At least in the short run, the poorest seem to suffer (or at least fail to gain in proportion to the rest of society) when countries move toward a market economy—unless government takes vigorous and wise corrective measures."[6] Added to the criticisms from these with a Christian orientation are many others around the world. For example, in a recent trip to London, just across the street from Westminster Abbey, I saw large banners assailing capitalism with statements such as, "Capitalism isn't working; another world is possible." We should note that these activists are able to express freely their sentiments because they live in a society that promotes freedom in religion, speech, and to some degree even economics. They do not seem to recognize the contradiction or at least the idealism in their thinking that government should control economies but allow them the freedom to speak out. Governments that control economies typically also control speech.

The questions before us then are these: Exactly what are capitalism and socialism? Is capitalism or some of its aspects inherently

---

[4]Dewi Hughes, *Power and Poverty* (Downers Grove: Inter-Varsity Press, 2008), 26. The back cover of the book states that Hughes is "theological adviser to Tearfund, an international relief organization based in London, and a member of the Lausanne Movement's Theological Working Group."

[5] Sider, 138.

[6] Ibid., 139.

immoral? Is socialism the answer? Does the Bible endorse or support in principle either system? Is God on the side of the poor, demanding a redistribution of wealth from those more well off?

DEFINITIONS

The Christian has the responsibility to search the Scriptures for principles and approved practices by which to analyze economic systems, with capitalism and socialism basic to all others. Capitalism is

> an economic system in which the greater proportion of economic life, particularly ownership of and investment in production goods, is carried on under private (i.e., nongovernmental) auspices through the process of economic competition and the avowed incentive of profit.[7]

In contrast, socialism is "any of the various economic and political theories advocating collective or governmental ownership and administration of the means of production and distribution of goods."[8] The *American Heritage Dictionary* gives a similar definition: "Any of various theories or systems of social organization in which the means of producing and distributing goods is owned collectively or by a centralized government that often plans and controls the economy."[9] The definitions vary slightly, but it seems accurate to say that consistent socialists agree generally on these three points: (1) property ownership should be collective rather than private; (2) the world's wealth should be distributed equally; (3) the profit motive is immoral because it allegedly encourages

---

[7] Julius Gould and William L. Kolb, eds. *A Dictionary of the Social Sciences* (New York: The Free Press of Glencoe, 1964).

[8] *Webster's New Collegiate Dictionary* (Springfield: G. and C. Merriam Company, 1975).

[9] *The American Heritage Dictionary of the English Language*, 4th ed. (Boston: Houghton Mifflin, 2002).

greed and unfairly high profits. A brief biblical analysis of these three areas will help us draw some conclusions regarding the way we should view economic systems and policies.

PROPERTY OWNERSHIP

Socialists' Attitude toward Private Property

The right of private property, that is, the right of individual ownership of property in all its forms, is central to capitalism.[10] Consequently the foes of capitalism oppose this right vehemently.[11] Karl Marx summed up the socialist theory in the pithy phrase: "the abolition of private property."[12] Some "Christian" socialists regard private property as robbery. For example, Henry C. Vedder states that private ownership of the "means of production" is "theft."[13] He even suggests that the abolition of "private capital," the motive for conflict, could help eliminate war.[14] Moreover, he recognizes that the socialists' goal of economic parity will eventually eliminate private property.[15] His reasoning is significant because he recognizes that the three major tenets of socialism—the abolition of private property, the worldwide equalization of wealth, and the elimination of the profit motive—rise or fall together.

---

[10] Robert B. McBurney, "Economics: Does It Matter Which System?" *Life's Answer*, April 1981, 16.

[11] Socialists object to private ownership of land and of the means of production. However, they normally do not object to the private ownership of smaller items such as clothes and furniture. Therefore, this section will focus on the right of private ownership of land and of the means of production. For the sake of conciseness, the term private property will hereafter denote the ownership of land, of animals, and of the means of production. This broad use of the term *property* is in keeping with the Old Testament concept of property. See John A. Battle, "Property Rights and Responsibilities in the Old Testament," *The Reformation Review*, XXVI (January 1981), 6–8.

[12] D. Ryanzanoff, ed., *The Communist Manifesto* (New York: Russell and Russell, 1963), 43.

[13] Henry C. Vedder, *Socialism and the Ethics of Jesus* (New York: Macmillan, 1912), 147–48.

[14] Ibid., 252.

[15] Ibid., 277.

Socialists have raised serious moral questions about capitalism and its associated right of ownership of private property. However, one must not accept their criticisms naively. The Christian's chief concern must be for the biblical attitude toward the private ownership of property.

Biblical Attitude toward Private Property

The biblical arguments for private property are basically two. The first argument is that the Scriptures present the private ownership of property as normal. Many biblical characters owned land. The second argument is that certain commands and moral precepts guarantee the right of private property. These commands prohibit stealing, require honesty in business dealings, and require the maintenance of the property of others.[16]

Examples of Private Ownership from the Old Testament

The Bible repeatedly approves private ownership. Because of its preponderance, biblical evidence must be used selectively rather than exhaustively. Although the following treatment is selective, it is sufficient to establish the biblical attitude toward the right of private ownership.

Job, one of the earliest biblical characters, held the right of property ownership. His possessions were vast. He owned "seven thousand sheep, and three thousand camels, and five hundred yoke of oxen, and five hundred she asses, and a very great household" (Job 1:3). No doubt he also owned much land, for he was the wealthiest of all the men in his part of the world (1:3). But even the figures in Job 1 do not tell the whole story, for Job later received double his original possessions (42:10–12). Since the Lord gave Job an abundance of property ("the Lord gave Job twice as much as he had

---

[16] John A. Battle (10–12) has suggested this threefold categorization of commands.

before," v. 10), one may infer that the Lord Himself sanctions individual ownership of property.

Individual ownership of land and of the means of production was common in the days of the patriarchs. Normally, the patriarchs were not large landholders, but they owned much of the means of production. In their society one who owned flocks and herds was an owner of the means of production. However, a wealthy owner like Abraham could also own land if he desired. On one occasion Abraham bought a burial ground for Sarah (Gen. 23). Although Abraham's nomadic lifestyle prevented him from becoming a large landowner, he and the men of his day regarded land ownership as a societal norm. The account of Abraham's transactions with Ephron treats the transfer of land ownership as a solemn matter.[17] Land ownership was a privilege and a right that deserved careful maintenance.

"And Judah and Israel dwelt safely, every man under his vine and under his fig tree, . . . all the days of Solomon" (1 Kings 4:25; cf. Micah 4:4; Zech. 3:10). This verse shows that private land ownership was common in Israel's monarchial era. One commentator aptly describes the scene as Micah presents it:

> It is the ideal of the peasant farmer freed from the demands and threats of the military state. . . . It is a very poignant, lovely, and real possibility that the farmer should live on *his* property and enjoy the result of his labour undisturbed [emphasis added].[18]

---

[17] Ephron, the son of Zohar, owned the land that Abraham bought (Gen. 23:8–9). When Ephron sold it, he officially "deeded over" the ownership to Abraham (Gen. 23:17–18, 20, NASB). They may have concluded this transaction by making a written contract on a cuneiform tablet. See Roland de Vaux's discussion of this possibility. *Ancient Israel*, 168.

[18] James Luther Mays, *Micah* (Philadelphia: The Westminster Press, 1976), 98.

Thus every man enjoys the fruit of his labor on his own land. Using the same imagery, Isaiah paints the millennial picture of private ownership even more graphically:

> And they shall build houses, and inhabit them; and they shall plant vineyards, and eat the fruit of them. They shall not build, and another inhabit; they shall not plant, and another eat: . . . and mine elect shall long enjoy the work of their hands (65:21–22).

Because millennial practices will exhibit God's ideal government of society, one may conclude that private ownership is part of His ideal. This biblical information alone furnishes adequate proof of God's approval of the private ownership of property.

The "virtuous woman" also enjoyed the fruit of her labor. With some of her profits she bought land and became a private landowner (Prov. 31:16). She had a right of private land ownership, for she worked efficiently, industriously, and honestly. God has only the highest praise for her (vv. 10, 28–31).

The prophet Jeremiah was also a private landowner. At the command of God, he purchased a field in Anathoth, a city within the confines of Jeremiah's tribe, Benjamin (Jer. 32:8). The Mosaic privilege of redemption permitted this purchase.[19] Apparently someone prepared a written deed of purchase, which Jeremiah sealed with his personal seal before several witnesses. The solemnity of the contractual procedure (32:10) again demonstrates the importance of private ownership.

The biblical prohibition of stealing (e.g., Ex. 20:15; Lev. 19:11) and the commands for honoring property boundaries (Deut. 19:14;

---

[19] See Lev. 25:24–25 for a statement of the Mosaic requirements. See Ruth 4:6–11 for an illustration of the fulfillment of the requirements by Boaz.

27:17; Prov. 22:28; 23:10) also teach that the right of private ownership is indisputable.

Examples of Private Ownership from the New Testament
Much of the Old Testament emphasis on private property relates to Israel's possession of the Promised Land. Nevertheless, others such as Abraham, Job, Jeremiah, and the "virtuous woman" illustrate the right of individual ownership of property apart from God's covenantal promises concerning Canaan. The Old Testament writers never questioned the right of owning private property. Likewise, the New Testament writers everywhere assume this right. They consider the individual ownership of land and of the means of production to be normal and proper.

For instance, Jesus based His parable of the hidden treasure (Matt. 13:44) upon one's right to buy and own property. The details of a parable do not establish doctrine, but they do illustrate economic practices in Christ's time. Jesus' parables are historically instructive because they "arise out of real situations."[20] "Part of their effectiveness," says New Testament scholar F. F. Bruce, "was due to their hearers' familiarity with the kind of situation described."[21] Therefore, private property and transactions regarding its sale and purchase were likely common in those days.[22]

The parable of the laborers in the vineyard also implies the right of private land ownership (Matt. 20:1–16).[23] As the master of his household, the owner of the vineyard had great authority. He

---

[20] A. M. Hunter, *Interpreting the Parables* (Philadelphia: The Westminster Press, 1960), 12.

[21] "Parable," *ZPEB* (1976), 4:595.

[22] According to Frederick C. Grand, even the peasants in Jesus' time owned little parcels of land that they had received by inheritance from allotments made in the Maccabean days or by older tribal rights. *The Economic Background of the Gospels* (New York: Russell and Russell, 1926), 64.

[23] Jesus also assumed this right in the parable of the rich fool (Luke 12:13–21).

had the right to use his property as he deemed best, as long as he treated his employees fairly. The major point of the parable depends on this right of a landowner to do what he wills with his own (v. 15).[24] We should note here also that this parable refutes the socialistic thinking that unless all workers receive the same pay, injustice has occurred. All of the workers received a fair wage for their work and in accordance with their verbal contract.

The fulfillment of an Old Testament prophecy also assumed the right of private land ownership. In fulfillment of Jeremiah's prophecy, the chief priests bought a potter's field with the money Judas had received for betraying Jesus (Matt. 27:3–10). Joseph of Arimathea further illustrates the right of land ownership that the men of his day enjoyed and that the writers of Scripture assumed. Joseph was a "rich man" (Matt. 27:57) who owned land near Jerusalem. Here again, the fulfillment of the Old Testament prophecy—"And he made his grave . . . with the rich in his death" (Isa. 53:9*a*)—assumes the right of private land ownership. If Joseph had not intervened with the Roman authorities, and if he had not owned a garden plot, the authorities would have buried Jesus with the two malefactors in an unmarked grave.

Peter's words to Ananias, "Whiles it remained, was it not thine own?" (Acts 5:4*a*) further prove that even in those days of communal concern, the right of private property remained valid. Ananias

---

[24] Having fulfilled his contract with the laborers, the landowner was not guilty of injustice, even though he did not give the same rate of pay to all. He had the right to reward the laborers as he wished. In this case he rewarded them on the basis of "fidelity to opportunity." This fidelity is the Christian's responsibility. The main point of the parable is that Jesus will reward Christians on the basis of their fidelity. G. Campbell Morgan, *The Parables and Metaphors of Our Lord* (New York: Fleming H. Revell, 1943), 115.

had the right to decide what to do with his property and with the money gained by selling it.[25] As F. F. Bruce well states,

> No compulsion had been laid on Ananias to sell his property. . . . The communalism of the primitive Jerusalem community was clearly quite voluntary. The piece of land belonged to Ananias; he could keep it or sell it as he pleased, and when he sold it, the money he got for it was his to use as he chose.[26]

Of course, connected with the right of private land ownership is always the privilege and responsibility of helping the Christian community as a "matter of individual conscience and free bounty."[27] Later evidence shows that John Mark's mother exercised her liberty and kept her house (Acts. 12:12). She helped the community by allowing Christians to gather there in what must have been a comparatively commodious house.

Paul's instructions about giving also indicate that the communal sharing of goods in Jerusalem did not continue.[28] Paul never intimated knowledge of any group of believers practicing a community of goods. Rather his epistles "presuppose the fact and the justification of private property."[29] Christian giving is in fact predicated upon the concept of personal ownership. Marvin Olasky, in his chapter "The Beginning of Hope" rightly points out, "Over and over again the Bible shows that there is no genuine giving

---

[25] "Power" (KJV) is best rendered "authority." The word (ἐξουσία) denotes the "power of decision." See the *Theological Dictionary of the New Testament* (1964), 2:566.

[26] F. F. Bruce, *Commentary on the Book of Acts* (Grand Rapids: Eerdmans, 1976), 113.

[27] Fenton John Anthony Hort, *The Christian Ecclesia* (New York: Macmillan and Co., 1898), 48.

[28] See, for example, 1 Cor. 16:2 and 2 Cor. 8 and 9.

[29] Orello Cone, *Rich and Poor in the New Testament* (New York: Macmillan, 1902), 151.

without self-reliance, based upon private property, at the disposal of the giver, earned by work, investment, or inheritance (a recognition of the work of forefathers)."[30]

Throughout the Bible the writers assume the right of ownership of private property. Usually they simply state that men and women, most of them godly, owned or purchased lands, houses, flocks, herds, and goods. The Gospel writers indicate that Jesus often based His parables on the right of individual land ownership. The writers of Scripture nowhere question this right. However, they indicate that a heavenly abode is the Christian's most important possession (Heb. 11:9, 13–16).

WEALTH DISPARITY

Besides questioning the validity of private ownership, some critics of capitalism have lambasted the way wealth is distributed in the world. They have been especially vociferous in blaming the affluent West and its so-called "structural injustices" for causing and perpetuating the misery of the world's poor. Recall the already cited charge by Dewi Hughes that "the way we live in luxury in the minority world while millions die in poverty could well make us liable for the blood of the poor before God."[31] Jim Wallis makes much of wealth disparity and the alleged injustice of it. Quoting from a Pelagian tract from early church times, he writes, "No one should own more than is necessary but everyone should have what they need. A few rich people are the reason why there are so many poor."[32] Similarly, Ronald Sider, in his chapter "Structural Injustice Today," makes this charge: "If God's Word is true, then all of us who dwell in affluent nations are trapped in sin. We have

---

[30] Marvin Olasky, Herbert Schlossberg, Pierre Berthoud, and Clark Pinnock, *Freedom, Justice, and Hope* (Westchester, IL: Crossway Books, 1988), 130.

[31] D. Hughes, *Power and Poverty*, 26.

[32] Wallis, *Rediscovering Values*, 116.

profited from systematic injustice—sometimes only half-knowing, sometimes only half-caring, and always half-hoping not to know. We are guilty of sin against God and neighbor."[33] This is strong, sweeping condemnation indeed and requires an answer.

Biblical Attitude toward Wealth Disparity

The biblical case for economic disparity has two themes. First, economic disparity is consistent with God's plan for the world. Some men will be rich, some will be poor, some will be in between, and some will be both rich and poor in their lifetime. God makes people different economically just as He does in all other aspects of life. This first section will also examine passages that seem to suggest a partial approval of the equalization of wealth. These passages qualify God's approval of economic disparity. The second section will be a critique of the welfare state, for the practical result of implementing economic equalization will always be a welfare state, that is, a situation where the government uses its power to redistribute wealth. This second section, then, will also deal with the biblical concept of welfare.

Wealth Disparity: Consistent with God's Plan

Several passages teach that wealth disparity is consistent with God's plan for the world. That some of God's choice servants were wealthy implies His approval of economic inequality. One of those choice servants was Abraham. He was "very rich in cattle, in silver, and in gold" (Gen. 13:2). Abraham's nephew, Lot, also had great possessions (Gen. 13:5–6). God gave these men great wealth. Abraham in particular could attribute his wealth to God's blessing upon him. Significantly, Abraham enjoyed affluence even when

---

[33] Sider, *Rich Christians*, 5th ed., 177.

many poor people dwelled in the land.[34] This man whose godly character earned for him the description "the friend of God" no doubt sympathized with the poor.[35] Nevertheless, he maintained his wealth while helping the poor. Moreover, while Abraham's wealth remained great, his favor with God increased.[36]

God did not recommend the equal distribution of wealth even among family members (Deut. 21:15–17). A man who had two wives, one loved and the other hated (21:15), and sons by those wives, could not arbitrarily divide his wealth. Nor could he divide it equally. The oldest son in the family automatically had the right of the firstborn to receive a double portion of the inheritance (vv. 16–17). Moreover, only sons had a right to this inheritance. These regulations concerning inheritances were binding only on Jews. Although the New Testament gives no indication that these rules of inheritance are binding today, the rules do suggest that God does not expect an equal distribution of wealth. If He did not require it in the family relationship, where the equal and fair treatment of children is normally a necessity, He does not require it in the world.

In one verse the Lord demolishes any objection to the thesis of this section. The Lord not only approves economic disparity, He is the author of it. As Hannah sang in her prayer, "The Lord maketh poor, and maketh rich" (1 Sam. 2:7*a*). Or, as Solomon states essentially the same truth, "The rich and poor meet together: the Lord is the maker of them all" (Prov. 22:2). Hannah celebrated God's

---

[34] Canaan must have been full of poor people, for only a few years before the reentry of Abraham and Lot, the land had experienced a "grievous" famine (Gen. 12:10).

[35] See 2 Chron. 20:7; Isa. 41:8; and James 2:23 for the designation of Abraham as God's friend.

[36] For evidence that Abraham's wealth remained great, see Gen. 23:16; 24:1, 53; and 25:5–6. For evidence that he increased in favor with God, see Gen. 17:1–9 and 22:15–18.

sovereign control of the economic status of men. The point is not that the rich have reason to boast; on the contrary, the Lord often reverses their prospects. The point is that the Lord causes these economic advances and reversals and that men and women should exult "in the Lord" (1 Sam. 2:1), not their status. Solomon elaborates on the fact of economic disparity. Although all men are equal in their natural relation to God and dependence upon Him for life and sustenance, all have different stations and circumstances in life.[37] All men are sinners before God, but not all have the same economic rank. Implicit in the teaching of Proverbs 22:2 is that both rich and poor stand on equal terms before God and must live in humble acknowledgment of that truth regardless of their relative wealth. While the verse teaches that God is in sovereign control of men's economic status, it is also true that "there is no hint here that the poor should not better themselves."[38] Concerning God's attitude toward human attempts at economic equalization, Bridges' remarks are direct and pertinent:

> In equality of rank, could men continue for a single day? Difference of mind and talents, industry, self-denial, Providences, would shake the balance before the morning was gone. God never meant to level the world, any more than the surface of the earth. The distinction of *rich and poor* still remains in His appointment and all attempts to sink it must end in confusion.[39]

Three verses (Luke 12:13–15) describe the episode that prompted Jesus to speak the parable of the rich fool (Luke 12:16–21). One of Jesus' hearers asked Him to intervene unilaterally in the division

---

[37] Bridges, *Proverbs*, 397.

[38] Peter A. Steveson, *A Commentary on Proverbs* (Greenville: Bob Jones University Press, 2001), 297.

[39] Bridges, 398.

of a family inheritance (v. 13). Jesus implied in His response that His mission was not to settle disputes about inheritances, but to deal with more important, spiritual matters (v. 14). The hearer's primary problem was not that he had received an injustice, but that he was covetous. Consequently, Jesus warned him and other hearers: "Take heed, and beware of covetousness: for a man's life consisteth not in the abundance of the things which he possesseth" (v. 15). Jesus' words teach that appeals for dividing the world's wealth may issue from a spirit of covetousness.[40] Rich and poor alike must remember that the things in life that really matter are not material possessions, but eternal matters—"things which are not seen" (2 Cor. 4:18). Socialists suggest that only the wealthy are greedy, but this verse demonstrates that those with little wealth can be equally greedy.

An underlying assumption of the parable of the talents is that people differ in many ways (Matt. 25:14–30). Although every person has certain God-given abilities, some people are more gifted than others. For instance, people differ economically in their abilities to earn and manage wealth. Some people can handle "ten talents" of money properly. Therefore, God gives them that much to administer. Others can properly manage only "one talent," and God consequently gives them only one talent. The basic assumption of this parable contradicts the proposal of equal income for all. Since people are not equal in their abilities and efforts, they should not be made equal in wealth.

Philippians 4:12 proves conclusively that Paul was not suggesting a communization of wealth in his instructions to the Corinthians

---

[40] Richard S. Wheeler charges that "most of the thrust toward equality today is rooted in covetousness; actual concern for the poor has little to do with it." *Pagans in the Pulpit* (New Rochelle, NY: Arlington House Publishers, 1974), 35. Ludwig von Mises makes the same charge. *Planning for Freedom* 3rd ed. (South Holland, IL: Libertarian Press, 1974), 137–40.

(2 Cor. 8:13–15). Paul certainly would not enjoin practices that he himself neglected. He had not practiced communal economy throughout his life. At times he had experienced poverty, and at other times he had experienced affluence. In both circumstances he learned the spiritual lesson of contentment. Either can produce contentment if one joyfully accepts the condition as God's will.

A seemingly forgotten verse in the Christian socialists' demand for economic justice for the poor is Christ's promise to every one of His people, rich or poor. Reading the books about their plight, the poor might think they have no hope apart from the intervention of the rich and powerful. However, every believer can claim the promise of Matthew 6:33 that the Lord will provide every legitimate need for life. Even a rich man, if he is godly, takes great comfort during times of personal economic uncertainty in the unqualified promise that the Lord will provide "all these things" if he will seek first His kingdom and His righteousness. Those who are relatively or even much poorer should not let anyone rob them of this promise, which says nothing about arbitrary poverty levels and has no link to government policies.

Wealth Disparity Adjustments

Although God allows and sometimes approves of economic disparity, He has occasionally limited it. However, God nowhere sanctions anything approaching absolute economic equality. Rather, He simply qualifies His approval of economic disparity with positive calls to remember the poor. Moreover, He limits the scope of all His instructions about reducing disparity to particular groups of believers.

The Year of Jubilee

Jubilee 2000 was founded in 1997 by mostly religious (and mostly Christian) organizations in order to issue a "call to cancel the unpayable debt that is crushing the world's poorest countries."[41] They chose the name based on the biblical year of Jubilee and claim that "the biblical wisdom . . . calls for periodic debt relief to begin to level the playing field at least a little."[42] In other words, they are applying the teaching regarding the year of Jubilee to international situations where relatively rich countries have loaned money to developing countries. In his own words, an advocate of Jubilee 2000 acknowledges that the issue is complex but still insists "on definitive debt cancellation as a moral imperative for reducing poverty."[43] Is this a correct application of Old Testament teaching? To answer this question, we need a careful look at the laws of the year of Jubilee.

God did ordain a limited equalization of wealth during the year of Jubilee (Lev. 25:8–34), every fiftieth year. That year began on the Day of Atonement, when trumpeters all over the land sounded a ram's horn (v. 9). After that, masters freed slaves, and purchased lands reverted to original owners (vv. 10, 13). The enforcement of this commandment secured a temporary, relatively equal distribution of land wealth among the Israelites. No doubt a main purpose for the legislation was to prevent excessive accumulations of wealth. However, one cannot appropriately apply the principle of the Jubilee system worldwide, because it was only for God's obedient people.[44] One would expect such a system in a theocracy but hardly in the society of today. The mass of unsaved people in the world have no concept of the stewardship responsibility upon

---

[41] Jim Wallis, *Faith Works: How to Live Your Beliefs and Ignite Positive Social Change* (New York: Random House, 2000), 296.

[42] Ibid., 298.

[43] Ibid., 300.

[44] The Israelites could not have a year of Jubilee if they disobeyed God, because disobedience would result in their being driven out of the land (Deut. 28:63–68).

which God based the Jubilee (v. 23).[45] Furthermore, the principle of the Jubilee could work only where land ownership and population were relatively static. In fact, it could work only where original ownership of land could be established. The Israelites became the original owners by "divine fiat," but no landowner today can make a claim of original ownership of land.[46]

Moreover, God instituted the Jubilee mainly for "tribal perpetuation."[47] Therefore, only the twelve tribes of Israel, dwelling in the Promised Land, could legitimately apply the principle of the Jubilee. The year of Jubilee could not work today. Its importance for Christians is mainly as a type of deliverance from the bondage of sin.[48] The only New Testament reference (Luke 4:19) uses it in this way when Jesus referred to the "favorable year of the Lord."[49]

Another major problem with assuming that the Jubilee proves God's endorsement of economic equalization is that some of the poorest people were not helped by it at all. Generally, the strangers or immigrants were among the poorer classes. However, they were unaffected by the Jubilee land laws. The Jubilee laws did not cancel their "interest-bearing debts."[50] The Jubilee helped some poor Israelites temporarily, but it did nothing for poor immigrants.

---

[45] God owns all property, but He allows man to use it. Part of man's stewardship responsibility is to eschew covetousness and to help the poor.

[46] David Chilton, *Productive Christians in an Age of Guilt-Manipulators*, 2nd ed. (Tyler, TX: Institute for Christian Economics: 1981), 171.

[47] Battle, 13.

[48] See Isa. 61:1–2 and Luke 4:18–19.

[49] "Concretely, the allusion is to the 'year of jubilee', the year of liberation among men appointed by Yahweh (Lv. 25) and now made symbolic of his own saving acts." I. Howard Marshall, *The Gospel of Luke* in *The New International Greek Testament Commentary* (Exeter, England: Paternoster Press, 1978), 184.

[50] Chilton, 174.

A final observation about the Jubilee laws is that they deal only with land and not with other aspects of wealth. For example, if a successful farmer "had excess grain which he kept in his granaries, it was not returnable. If he sold all the produce he did not consume and stored away gold or silver instead of goods, he did not return any silver or gold—only land. There was no provision for a return of animals either."[51]

The Jerusalem Church

No one can deny that the early church in Jerusalem manifested a communal spirit (Acts 2:43–47; 4:34–5:11). Two verses in particular sum up the communal practice of this church: "And all that believed were together, and had all things common; and sold their possessions and goods, and parted them to all men, as every man had need" (2:44–45). Although these verses portray a community of sharing, they lend no support to the socialists' theory of universal economic equality. In reality, the verses soundly refute the socialistic idea.

First, the New Testament community of goods comprised only Christian members. Socialists demand that Christians and non-Christians alike give and take wealth in order to achieve worldwide parity. But the participants in this community of goods were all professing Christians.[52] No evidence suggests that they should have allowed unbelievers under their umbrella of mutual sharing. Besides, such mutual sharing could work only among those actuated by God's great grace and filled with the Holy Spirit (4:31–33).

In the second place, the early Christians *voluntarily* participated in the communal economy. Socialists may envision a society of voluntary sharing, but in practice, their system depends upon

---

[51] Harold Lindsell, *Free Enterprise: A Judeo-Christian Defense* (Wheaton: Tyndale House Publishers, 1982), 58.

[52] "All that *believed* [emphasis added] were together" (v. 44a).

coercion. Socialism cannot exist in a sin-cursed world unless government forces its citizens to divide their wealth.[53] In contrast, the members of the church in Jerusalem voluntarily shared their goods. Although this practice did begin to reduce the gap between rich and poor, it did not establish absolute equality. The procedure mentioned (4:34) was actually a process. The rich believers did not simultaneously sell their lands and houses. As needs arose, they were making sales and were bringing the proceeds to the apostles for distribution.[54] Although all may have been willing to sell their property, we know that not all did; Mark's mother, for example, continued to own a large house (Acts 12:12).

Paul's Exhortation to the Corinthians

Paul also mentioned a situation in which God seemingly limits economic disparity. Explaining his exhortation to complete the collection for the poor saints in Jerusalem, Paul told the Corinthian believers,

> I mean not that other men be eased, and ye burdened: but by an equality, that now at this time your abundance may be a supply for their want, that their abundance also may be a supply for your want: that there may be equality: as it is written, He that had gathered much had nothing over; and he that had gathered little had no lack (2 Cor. 8:13–15).

---

[53] The words *coercion* and *force* do not necessarily imply physical action. Socialism forces the redistribution of wealth in a number of ways, but mainly through high taxes upon the rich and welfare programs. See Marx's plan for carrying out his communism for other methods of redistribution. D. Ryazanoff, ed., *The Communist Manifesto*, 52–53. See also Ronald Sider's proposals in his chapter "Structural Change" in *Rich Christians*.

[54] R. C. H. Lenski, *The Interpretation of the Acts of the Apostles* (Columbus: The Wartburg Press, 1944), 189–90.

Paul advocated an "equality," but not the kind of equality that socialists propose. Paul's equality differs in several respects. First, whereas socialism is a program for all men, regardless of their religion, Paul's words apply only to the Christian brotherhood.[55] He was describing what can happen between Christians when they first give themselves completely to the Lord (2 Cor. 8:5). Secondly, whereas socialism demands economic equality, Paul makes it voluntary. He did not command (2 Cor. 8:8) but recommended an economy that is to their "advantage" (8:10*a*, NASB). Moreover, he encouraged only the willing ones to give (8:12). Paul's concept of equality differs from that of socialists, finally, in that it is not absolute. Paul suggests only a partial leveling of material holdings. He was concerned simply that the poor brethren in Jerusalem have their needs met. Hodge has rightly judged that "the equality . . . intended is not an equality as to the amount of property, but equal relief from the burden of want."[56] Paul recognized that economic forces are dynamic and inconstant. Those who are rich now may be poor later (v. 14). The socialistic ideal of the "communization of wealth" is impracticable as well as unbiblical.[57]

Biblical Concept of Welfare

The Role of Government

Although some socialists might not admit it, socialism is essentially a welfare state.[58] A dictionary of the social sciences lists the establishment of a "Welfare State" brought about by a "large-scale

---

[55] This point has already been made, but from a different passage. See above under "The Year of Jubilee" and "The Jerusalem Church." Nowhere does the Bible enjoin a reciprocity of giving in times of affluence and poverty between the saved and the unsaved.

[56] Hodge, *Second Epistle to the Corinthians*, 205.

[57] Philip Edgcumbe Hughes, *Paul's Second Epistle to the Corinthians*, 310.

[58] One socialist disavows that socialism is the same thing as the welfare system because the welfare state is too capitalistic. He claims that the unwillingness of the welfare state to take a position on the ownership of the means of production "betrays

extension of the social services" as a tenet acceptable to most socialists.[59] The distribution of wealth according to need necessitates a welfare state.[60] When one removes the rose of the socialistic ideal, one always finds the thorns of a welfare state. The essential equivalence of a welfare state and socialism is undeniable. Webster defines a welfare state as "a social system based upon the assumption by a political state of primary responsibility for the individual and social welfare of its citizens."[61] But that is socialism exactly, for in it too the state assumes the responsibility for its individuals' welfare.[62] About this role of the state in socialism, socialists are misleading. They euphemize about the "collective ownership of all means of production by all the members of the society."[63] But in reality the government would have to own all the means of production and control all industry.[64] "The people" will not manage the industries; the state leaders will. The potential danger of governmental control of the economy shows up clearly in the Antichrist's rule (Rev. 13). When he heads the political coalition of the world, he will also control the economy of the world (vv. 16–17). Those who will not cooperate with him will die (Rev. 13:15).

---

its essential capitalist orientation." William R. Coats, *God in Public: Political Theology Beyond Niebuhr* (Grand Rapids: Eerdmans, 1974), 179–80.

[59] Julius Gould and William L. Kolb, eds. *A Dictionary of the Social Sciences* (New York: The Free Press of Glencoe, 1964).

[60] Coats (182) praises the concept of "the distribution of wealth on the basis of need rather than in accord with the power, capital, or property of certain individuals or classes."

[61] *Webster's New Collegiate Dictionary* (Springfield: G. and C. Merriam Company, 1975).

[62] One socialist describes the government's role this way: "Socialism simply means making the nation the company." Fred Henderson, *The Case for Socialism* (Los Angeles: Levin and Weisenberg, n.d.), 42.

[63] Washington Gladden, *Christianity and Socialism* (New York: Eaton and Mains, 1905), 104.

[64] Ibid., 106.

Socialism makes the government responsible for the welfare of the people. However, the Bible refutes the principles of the welfare state.[65] First, the Bible limits the responsibility and therefore the power of government to the maintenance of law and order.[66] Nowhere does the New Testament suggest that the state should dole out money for the hungry or unemployed.[67] Individuals, instead, should relieve the poor.[68] When governments take the role of dispensing welfare, they may do more harm than good. One writer claims that "welfare state policies intended for the poor primarily increase the material well-being of the administering bureaucracies. The rhetoric may be social justice, but the reality is economic payoffs to the politically favored."[69] Furthermore, the Bible ranks one's welfare responsibilities. The Christian must first provide for his family (2 Cor. 12:14b; 1 Tim. 5:8, 16), then for other believers (Acts 6:1–3; Rom. 15:26; Gal. 6:10b; 1 Tim. 5:9–10; James 2:15–16; 1 John 3:17) and then for all men (Luke 10:25–37; Gal. 6:10a; Eph. 4:28).[70]

Though it seems straightforward enough, this analysis of one's welfare responsibilities does not begin to satisfy some evangelicals.

---

[65] A rector in the Episcopal Church, T. Robert Ingram, has written a trenchant critique of socialism. *The World under God's Law: Criminal Aspects of the Welfare State* (Houston: St. Thomas Press, 1962). He shows how socialism, or the welfare state (he uses the terms synonymously), contradicts each of the Ten Commandments.

[66] See Rom. 13:1–7 and 1 Pet. 2:13–14.

[67] Even in Egypt under Joseph the people had to pay for their food (Gen. 41:56).

[68] See, e.g., Acts 20:35; Gal. 2:10; Eph. 4:28.

[69] Clark H. Pinnock, "The Pursuit of Utopia," in *Freedom, Justice, and Hope* (Westchester, IL: Crossway Books, 1988), 78.

[70] Paul's admonition to the Galatians, "As we have therefore opportunity, let us do good unto all men, especially unto them who are of the household of faith" (6:10), proves the gradation of the Christian's welfare responsibilities. Of course, as he is able the Christian must use the opportunities afforded him to do good to all men. William Hendriksen makes the appropriate analogy between the parent's responsibility first to children and then to neighbors, and the Christian's responsibility first to Christians and then to all people. *New Testament Commentary: Exposition of Galatians* (Grand Rapids: Baker, 1968), 238.

For example, in March of 2011 *Sojourners* took out a full-page ad published on the Politico website. Regarding the current debate about the federal budget, it asked the question, "What Would Jesus Cut?" The ad claims that the budget is a "moral document" and that the "budget should not be balanced on the backs of poor and vulnerable people."[71] That sounds pious and compassionate, but consider Roger Pilon's reasoned answer to the assertion of *Sojourners* and others.

> They ask, implicitly, how "we" should spend "our" money, as though we were one big family quarreling over our collective assets. We're not. We're a constitutional republic, populated by discrete individuals, each with our own interests. Their question socializes us and our wherewithal. The Framers' Constitution freed us to make our own individual choices. . . . The ads' signers imagine that the Good Samaritan parable instructs us to attend to the afflicted through the coercive government programs of the modern welfare state. It does not. The Good Samaritan is virtuous not because he helps the fallen through force of law but because he does so voluntarily, which he can do only if he has the right to freely choose the good, or not. . . . Today the federal government exercises vast powers never granted to it, restricting liberties never surrendered. It's all reflected in the federal budget, the redistributive elements of which speak to nothing so much as theft – and that's immoral.[72]

The Role of Work

Work is basic to the biblical concept of welfare. The Christian's primary social responsibility is to work so as not to burden others

---

[71] The ad can be seen at http://www.sojo.net/special/politico.html. Accessed May 4, 2011.

[72] "Is It Immoral to Cut the Budget?" *The Wall Street Journal*, 7 April 2011, sec. A, p. 17.

(Eph. 4:28; 1 Thess. 4:11–12; 2 Thess. 3:7–12). Although socialists claim that their system requires every man to work, in practice a welfare state destroys incentive to work.[73] Socialists might tell people to work hard and nobly, but the poor have little incentive when they know that some method of governmental economic leveling will fill their pockets. Furthermore, the rich have little incentive to work when they know that their pockets will be emptied. These editorial remarks expose the deadening effect of welfarism:

> Once it is established that the majority has the right to dispossess the minority, the process will go on and on until the last taxpayer has been picked bare and there is no incentive anywhere to work hard and produce abundantly. Production therefore declines and in time there are no haves for the have-nots to dispossess. In the end the welfare state will have nothing but poverty to distribute.[74]

Socialists propose a welfare state partially because they misunderstand the causes of poverty. One socialist claims that the poor are "locked in their stations by bourgeois prejudice and economic capitalism."[75] Another implies that American prosperity causes "poverty and starvation abroad."[76] Karl Marx blames capitalist employers for the poverty of laborers. He claims,

> The capitalist gets rich, not like the miser, in proportion to his personal labour and restricted consumption, but at the same rate as he squeezes out the labour-power of

---

[73] Henry C. Vedder (277) claims that one of the two basal principles of socialism is that "every man must work."

[74] Editorial, "The Future of the Welfare State," *Christian Economics*, XVIII (February 22, 1966), 2.

[75] Coats, 134.

[76] Ronald J. Sider, "A Call for Evangelical Nonviolence," *The Christian Century* (September 15, 1976), 757.

others, and enforces on the labourer abstinence from all life's enjoyments.[77]

In other words, capitalism causes poverty because the managerial class exploits the laboring class. In essence, some socialists blame capitalism for poverty. They have difficulty admitting that poverty can have other causes besides capitalist exploitation.

Reasons for Poverty

Contrary to socialist thought, the Scriptures teach that some people bring poverty on themselves. For example, Solomon indicated that lazy people invite poverty. He warned the drowsy sluggard, "So shall thy poverty come as one that travelleth, and thy want as an armed man" (Prov. 6:11).[78] Moreover, he observed that "he becometh poor that dealeth with a slack hand" (Prov. 10:4a). Solomon also suggested that stingy people ironically tend to become poor. The possessions of stingy givers are apt to decrease. In other words, stinginess "tendeth to poverty" (Prov. 11:24). Others who will likely experience poverty are those who live for pleasure, particularly heavy drinkers and gluttons. Solomon warns them that "he that loveth pleasure shall be a poor man: he that loveth wine and oil shall not be rich" (Prov. 21:17). Solomon further admonished his readers, "Do not be with heavy drinkers of wine, or with gluttonous eaters of meat; for the heavy drinker and the glutton will come to poverty" (Prov. 23:20–21a, NASB). Finally, the wasteful deserve poverty. The example of the prodigal son illustrates well how wasteful living can bring one to abject poverty (Luke 15:11–17). The prodigal knew that his poverty was self-inflicted (vv. 18–19). So all of these—the lazy, the stingy, the epicurean, and the wasteful—deserve poverty. They have no

---

[77] Karl Marx, *Capital*, ed. Frederick Engels (New York: The Modern Library, 1906), 651.

[78] Cf. Prov. 24:34. See also 20:13.

legitimate claim to the beneficence of others. In fact, beneficence would harm rather than help them, for they would misuse it. Socialists propose economic equality for all and thus overlook the necessity for wise judgment in giving to the poor. However, the Bible applauds such discernment.[79]

In reviewing the data surveyed thus far, we must also acknowledge that some reasons for poverty are simply beyond our purview. Recall that Solomon wrote that the Lord is the maker of both rich and poor (Prov. 22:2). Job's experience and Ecclesiastes teach the same truth. Blomberg summarizes nicely: "Job and Ecclesiastes remind us that the reasons some are poor or rich remain locked in the mysteries of God."[80]

THE PROFIT MOTIVE

Those who have a socialist orientation are quick to point out the supposed greed of entrepreneurs. They claim in particular that larger companies (they often call them MNCs—multinational corporations) exploit people by giving them low wages and prices for their resources "far below Western market values," all the while making an exorbitant profit.[81] The practical problem with their charges is that companies have to make a profit to survive and provide jobs for people. The biblical problem with their charges is that the Bible recognizes this fact and approves of legitimate profit making.

---

[79] The Lord does not necessarily give to Christians everything they desire, for sometimes they desire to "spend" on their own "pleasures" (James 4:3, NASB). Christians should adopt the same principle. They should not give money to those who will obviously use it to fuel their sin.

[80] *Neither Poverty Nor Riches*, 82.

[81] Wallis, *The Call to Conversion*, 44–45.

Biblical Examples

The example of the "virtuous woman" validates the right to make an honest profit. As a result of her diligent labor, this woman has surplus money. She makes a profit, and a handsome profit at that. With her profits she brings some of the food for her household from distant countries (Prov. 31:14). She also buys property, which she has carefully considered and found to be advantageous to her (v. 16). She even has enough money left over to provide clothing of high quality for her household and herself (vv. 21–22). In every way she is enterprising. She is not embarrassed because she makes a profit, for she knows that her profit is an important means to several ends. One of her goals is to provide adequately for her female servants (v. 15). Her example proves that an employer can make a personal profit and still honorably provide for employees. Another of her goals is to broaden her base of business (v. 16), and another is to provide the best nutrition and clothing for herself and her family (vv. 14, 21–22, 27*a*). But she is not selfish, for another goal is to provide for the needy (v. 20). Plainly, her making of profit is good because it enables her to better her own, her family's, and her acquaintances' condition.

Lydia's manner of profiting also proves that private profit is legitimate. Apparently Lydia, "a seller of purple, of the city of Thyatira" (Acts 16:14*a*), was Paul's first convert in Philippi. Like the virtuous woman, Lydia stands out as a successful businesswoman. Inscriptions and scrolls from that time indicate the existence in Thyatira of a guild of traders in purple-dyed cloth.[82] As an agent sent out from a firm back in Thyatira, Lydia must have been a woman of some means. The products she bought were expensive and would

---

[82] Herbert Lockyer, *All the Trades and Occupations of the Bible* (Grand Rapids: Zondervan, 1969), 286.

have required considerable capital.[83] Although she was wealthy, nothing in the account suggests that she was "addicted" to greed or a "competitive individualism." Rather than rebuking her for her wealth, Paul enjoyed the hospitality that her wealth offered him and his company (16:15).

Like Lydia, Paul and his friends Aquila and Priscilla also worked for a profit. While in Corinth, Paul was the employee of a tent-making business owned by Aquila and Priscilla. According to a description by F. F. Bruce, this business operated on capitalistic principles. He describes the couple and the business operation:

> They appear to have been a well-to-do couple, and their tent-making business may have had branches in several centres, with a manager in charge of the branches in those places where they themselves were not actually resident. They were thus able to move back and forth easily between Rome, Corinth and Ephesus.[84]

Thus Aquila and Priscilla were most likely entrepreneurs. They had a profitable business, and they channeled some of their profits for the expansion of their business. Their government did not control their business. But Aquila and Priscilla were devout Christians as well as successful entrepreneurs. They were among Paul's most loyal friends through the years—years in which they apparently remained in the tent-making business. A few years after this time with them in Corinth, Paul expressed his appreciation for their faithfulness to him and for their service to "all the churches of the Gentiles" (Rom. 16:4).[85] Thus Aquila, Priscilla, and Paul exemplified

---

[83] Ibid., 287.

[84] F. F. Bruce, *Paul: Apostle of the Heart Set Free* (Grand Rapids: Eerdmans, 1977), 250–51.

[85] For other references to them and their dedication to serving the Lord, see Acts 18:26–27; 1 Cor. 16:19; and 2 Tim. 4:19.

the proper capitalist spirit. Although they profited in their business, they did not neglect the work of the Lord. Contrarily, every indication suggests that their success in business enabled them to serve the Lord better. For example, the prosperity of Aquila and Priscilla provided them with a home in which they gladly accommodated a local church (Rom. 16:5). In summary, then,

> They made money, but it was that they might spend it for God. This is one of the way-marks of Christian trading all down the centuries. The story of the coincidence between spiritual fullness and commercial success is one of the phenomena of history which no sneers should be permitted to vulgarise.[86]

Indeed, those who assail the motive of making a profit must question the character of Paul, Aquila, Priscilla, and ultimately God, for the three tentmakers profited, and God blessed their efforts as He has blessed those of His devoted and enterprising people through the years.

Warnings about Greed

As we have seen, several biblical references validate the profit motive. Of course, the Scripture writers legitimate neither profit as an end in itself, nor every means of making a profit. They balance the right to make a profit with warnings against the inordinate pursuit of it. Proverbs furnishes several of these warnings. For example, the writer condemns those who exploit poor people by withholding grain in seasons of scarcity in order to drive prices higher (Prov. 11:26). The writer warns further about being "greedy of gain" (Prov. 15:27a). The person who unjustly and greedily acquires wealth ruins himself and his family. Therefore, Solomon

---

[86] Harrington C. Lees, *St. Paul's Friends* (London: The Religious Tract Society, 1917), 62.

also admonishes, "Labour not to be rich" (Prov. 23:4a). The pursuit of profit above all else is vain. One should cease from inordinately pursuing that which, though apparently within one's grasp, will always elude it.[87] Finally, Agur suggests the safest attitude toward profit in his broad comments about material possessions (Prov. 30:8–9). The individual should be content with a profit that categorizes him as neither poor nor wealthy. A person has fewest temptations when he has only what is sufficient for his needs.

Some of the prophets also warn against the inordinate pursuit of profit. Isaiah inveighed against those who monopolized landholdings for profit (5:8; cf. Micah 2:2). However, he did not condemn the right to purchase property, but rather the monopolistic acquisition of what belonged to a poor owner.[88] The actions of the monopolists revealed their covetousness and selfishness. These attitudes pervert the motive of profit. Jeremiah follows Isaiah in rebuking those who profit unfairly (22:13–14). He singles out King Jehoiakim, who profited at the expense of his subjects. By making his subjects work for no pay, Jehoiakim was able to build elaborate royal edifices. Amos, too, condemns those who economically oppress the poor (Amos 8:4–8). Some of his contemporaries craved profit so much that they disliked religious days, because on those days they could do no business. They also cheated the poor with "dishonest scales" (8:5, NASB). We should note, however, that the prophets were attacking the sins that issue from the heart and not the system itself. Griffiths is right:

> The prophets indict the rich for exploiting the poor. Yet they never suggest that the remedy is therefore an economic redistribution conducted in some sort of spiritual

---

[87] See the simile in Prov. 23:5 which likens the stability of wealth to the flight of an eagle.

[88] E. J. Young, *The Book of Isaiah* (Grand Rapids: Eerdmans, 1965), 1:206.

vacuum. They invariably pinpoint the root cause of the trouble as spiritual: the nation has departed from God and economic injustice is one result. The priority therefore is not socio-economic reform but spiritual repentance.[89]

But it is just this kind of misapplication of the indictment that some well-meaning writers make. For example, applying Jeremiah's condemnation of Jehoiakim's greed, Hughes makes this sweeping charge: "Power in the hands of the greedy means poverty. In a world where 20% of its people own 80% of its wealth, it is difficult to avoid the conclusion that the 20% are greedy."[90] Such statements are unhelpful and unprovable. Does greed then stop at the top 20%?

The New Testament writers continue the warnings about the unbridled or dishonest pursuit of profit. Matthew suggests that he who pursues profit to the neglect of eternal salvation will lose eternally (16:26). The story of the rich fool in Luke 12:16–21 reinforces this point. Although the man made great profits (vv. 16–19), he pursued wealth rather than godliness (vv. 20–21). Such an inordinate pursuit of profit is the height of folly. Paul too warns the Christian about this love of money. He states that the love of money and the desire to be rich has caused many to stray from biblical truth and practice and to suffer numerous sorrows (1 Tim. 6:9–10).

Finally, James warned against the arrogant pursuit of commercial profit (4:13–16). However, James's words do not forbid the normal practices of business—buying, selling, and getting gain (v. 13). Although he denounced the presumptuous businessmen who forgot that God rules men's affairs, he did not condemn profit. Rather,

---

[89] Brian Griffiths, *The Creation of Wealth* (Downers Grove: InterVarsity, 1984), 60.

[90] D. Hughes, *Power and Poverty*, 184.

he admonished every businessman to recognize God's sovereignty over profits and losses. The businessman should say, "If the Lord so wills, I will go into a city and there make a profit" (v. 15). So James did not condemn enterprising businessmen or the profits they gained from honest trade. But he did condemn a "presumptuous disregard of God's will."[91] Merchants thus can be godly. The presumptuous merchant should forsake his audacity, not his business.

We have seen that while the inordinate pursuit of wealth is a grave danger, the honest pursuit of profit is fully acceptable. Indeed, profit is the dynamic of any economy. Without it, even socialistic economies will stagnate and die. No wonder then that God in His wisdom supports the ownership of property, the enjoyment of one's portion of wealth given by God, and the making of profit to keep companies producing and people fruitfully employed.

Paul and others made a profit, but these godly believers also kept in mind their stewardship responsibilities. Paul said regarding the exhortation from the Jerusalem church leaders to "remember the poor," that this was "the very thing I also was eager to do" (Gal. 2:10, NASB). Paul exhibited the proper biblical perspective. We should be free to work and earn wealth, but at all times we must remember that God has blessed us so we can be a blessing to others, especially to those in need.

When all the biblical warnings, examples, and instructions regarding wealth are digested and summarized, one desiring to please the Lord with his wealth can do nothing better than to join Agur in praying, "Give me neither poverty nor riches; feed me with the food that is my portion, that I not be full and deny You and say, 'Who is the Lord?' Or that I not be in want and steal, and profane the name of my God" (Prov. 30:8–9, NASB).

---

[91] D. Edmond Hiebert, *The Epistle of James* (Chicago: Moody Press, 1979), 275.

Conclusion

We live in a day when the ideas of moral absolutes and biblical certainties are almost universally questioned. Modern thinking about these issues is often poll-driven. The pollsters frame the questions, and the media faithfully pass along the findings. Moral issues are never black and white but subject to the manipulated thinking of the masses. For example, many now view abortion and homosexuality favorably. On a matter related to the content of this book, we now know from one survey that

> overall more Americans believe that Christian values are at odds with capitalism and the free market than believe they are compatible. This pattern also holds among Christians. Among Christians in the U.S., only 38% believe capitalism and the free market are consistent with Christian values while 46% believe the two are at odds.[1]

So presumably the majority of Christians in America would disagree with chapter 6 in this book. On the other hand, how many of them have had the opportunity to examine carefully what the Scriptures actually say about the issues related to capitalism, or even about tithing or saving or indebtedness? The opportunity to examine the Scriptures carefully about these topics and to present those findings is precisely the thrust of this short book. The answers to questions about how a Christian should think about and handle money should not come from surveys of public opinion, however professionally conducted. The answers must come from the only source of pure wisdom, the unchanging Word of God.

---

[1] http://www.publicreligion.org/research/?id=554.

Riches are uncertain and unstable but to some extent indispensable. Because they are both necessary and dangerous, it behooves us to establish biblical certainties regarding them. We do not need to know what the public thinks in the latest poll; we need to know what God has said in His lasting Book. Once that is known, the only acceptable answer for the Bible believer is "completely agree."